D0913122

Existentialism

This book is one of a series, Traditions in Philosophy, published by Pegasus in cooperation with Educational Resources Corporation, which has developed and created the series under the direction of Nicholas Capaldi, Professor of Philosophy, Queens College, New York.

About the Author

Patricia F. Sanborn, assistant professor of philosophy at the University of New Mexico, has taught at Barnard College and at Hunter College. A graduate of Mount Holyoke College, she received her M.A. and Ph.D. degrees from Columbia University.

Existentialism

by Patricia F. Sanborn

PEGASUS   NEW YORK

To David Leonard

Preface

This book is designed as a general introduction to Existentialism, through a study of five major figures in the movement. It is organized around traditional philosophical topics, in an attempt to indicate continuities in the thought of the Existentialists and to show the relationship of their positions to the history of Western philosophy. It is hoped that this book will be read in conjunction with primary sources. There is no substitute for a direct encounter with the writings of the men with whom it is concerned.

One difficulty in writing a book on Existentialism is that of consolidating the material without distorting it. The diversity of style and subject matter in the writings of the Existentialists often creates obstacles to a coherent presentation of the ideas. For this reason two approaches to the material are used. On some issues the philosophers are considered separately because of variations in the positions that they take. This is the procedure used, for the most part, in the chapters on theory of knowledge.

In other parts of the discussion, material from some or all of the philosophers is grouped together, incorporating the features that are held in common. This method is used in parts of the chapters on ethics and social philosophy. In other chapters, both methods are used. Because of limits of space, not all philosophers are considered in the analysis of each topic. Those discussed have been chosen as representative.

The materials used in this study are available in translation. Two major works have yet to be translated—Jaspers' *Philosophie,* which appeared in 1932, and Sartre's *Critique de la raison dialectique,* which was published in 1961. Reference is made only to the portions of these works that have been translated. Bibliographical information is oriented towards texts that are available in paperback editions. The terminology used here is that of the standard translations, except in situations in which one word has been translated in different ways. In such cases, I have used the translation which is, in my opinion, the most successful. In the occasional references to untranslated material, the translation which is provided is my own.

The writing of this book was assisted by a grant from the Research Allocations Fund of the University of New Mexico. I also wish to thank Mr. and Mrs. Eugene Urbain and Eugene S. Urbain for their contribution to the preparation of the manuscript.

Patricia F. Sanborn
Albuquerque, New Mexico

Contents

Existentialism

1

Introduction

The Origins

Existentialism can claim to have attracted more attention from nonphilosophers than any other recent philosophical movement. Yet as a philosophical movement, it is not unique. The history of philosophy lends itself to groupings of philosophers. Sometimes these groupings point to the mutual interaction of philosophers; sometimes they isolate those thinkers who have a basic philosophical stance in common. The Existentialist movement falls most readily into the latter category. In the major writings of the Existentialists, similarities of method and argument emerge. The Existentialists react in common against their philosophical heritage. It is, perhaps, the force of this reaction against the past that has gained this movement much of the attention it has received.

With a group of philosophers as diverse as those under discussion, it is not always easy to point to common features. A few of the thinkers who will be considered here have disavowed the label of "Existentialist" at some point in their careers. The popular following of the French Existentialists, and the fringe groups that have appropriated the terminology of the Existentialists, are partially responsible for the refusal of some serious philosophers to ally themselves directly with the Existentialist movement.

The immediate historical roots of Existentialism are found in the middle of the nineteenth century, when Søren Kierkegaard (1813–1855) was writing in Denmark. Generally considered to be the "father" of the movement, Kierkegaard presents the first consistent statement of the principles that are crystallized in the writings of the twentieth century. Although one often finds the name of Friedrich Nietzsche (1844–1900) mentioned in conjunction with that of Kierkegaard, it is Kierkegaard who has had the more direct influence on subsequent Existentialism.

In the twentieth century four figures stand out: Martin Heidegger (1889–＿＿), Karl Jaspers (1883–＿＿), Gabriel Marcel (1889–＿＿), and Jean-Paul Sartre (1905–＿＿). It is with these four, along with Kierkegaard, that this book will be mainly concerned. The ideas of a number of peripheral figures will be cited to illustrate specific points, but the five philosophers noted will serve as the principle sources of material. They exemplify the central branches of the movement and have developed their ideas extensively in philosophical form.

Many of the concepts introduced by the Existentialists have found their way into fields other than philosophy. Figures as varied as Dostoevsky, Rilke, and Jean Genet have been called Existentialists. In such cases one or more of the themes of the Existentialist philosophies can be found in their writings, yet it does not follow that these themes have been borrowed directly from the philosophical movement. Such concerns have been pervasive in the arts long before the appearance of Existentialism as an articulated philosophy.

The question can be posed as to how much interaction there is between the central figures of the movement. To some extent, all of the more recent Existentialist writers acknowledge their debt to Kierkegaard. Yet there is considerable independence in the development of ideas. The closest link is that which was formed between Heidegger and Sartre, but even that connection is none too strong in the light of Sartre's many criticisms of Heidegger's thought. Marcel makes a comment about his own work that could apply equally well to the work of all of the others. He claims that his thought developed independently of the thought of the others, and that the discovery of similarities came late and somewhat unexpectedly in his philosophical career. The similarities that do occur can be attributed to a simultaneous emergence of like concerns.

One factor that the Existentialists hold in common is external—their geographical location. The movement gathered force and culled its major representatives from continental Europe. For the most part, the Anglo-Saxon world has not been attracted to the movement with the intensity of the continental European intellectual community. There are, however, two exceptions: Existential psychoanalytic theory and Protestant theology in the United States. The foremost representative of the Protestant theologians, the late Paul Tillich, was educated in Germany but made extensive contributions to American theological thought.[1]

Related, perhaps, to the geographical factor is a common interest in political activity. The commitments, however, are far from uniform. There have been variations as wide as Sartre's link to Marxism and Marcel's affiliation with the moral rearmament movement. To some extent the political affiliations of these thinkers are related to their philosophical positions. These relationships will be explored in more detail in Chapter VI.

Another external similarity between them is the fact that most of them have either written plays or novels or have been literary critics. Heidegger and Marcel offer extensive analyses of poets; Sartre and Marcel have written plays. Sartre is the author of numerous short stories and novels, and Kierkegaard's writings include considerable literary criticism. The interest that a number of the Existentialists have in the arts suggests the strong interdisciplinary flavor of their concerns.

Such literary activity can be interpreted in a number of ways. It is impossible to explore here the implications of the extensive nonphilosophical output of these thinkers.[2] This work indicates a broad conception of the function of the philosopher. He does not exist in isolation from other creative disciplines. Not only does he study these disciplines; he also participates in them. In addition, the philosophical ideas of the Existentialists lend themselves readily to concrete embodiment in drama and other art forms. The emphasis on concreteness, individuality, and personal experience, of course, was formerly thought of as the province of artists rather than philosophers.

Perhaps even more to the point than the external similarities between these thinkers are the internal similarities— those which appear directly in the ideas developed. One common feature is rebellion: rebellion against the apathy and slumber of the intellectuals; rebellion against the insensitivity of colleagues; and rebellion against the inhumanity and irrelevance of institutions such as the church, the state, and the university. Behind these rebellions is the conviction that many aspects of the environment suffocate the individual. Kierkegaard sees his struggle against the Church of Denmark as a struggle for the very air of survival. The world around is interpreted as a hostile one, in which the concrete individual is lost. It is a world that has lost sight of the paradoxical elements of man.

One of the tasks that the Existentialists set themselves is that of understanding the individual who has been hidden in the "untruth" of the crowd.[3] The human condition must be described in terms that are real and concrete, and the first subject of concern is the person who does the describing. This is not the self as one wishes it to be, nor is it some preestablished ideal self. It is the limited, incomplete, here-and-now self, an individual aspiring to a personal concrete destiny. In a crowd the sense of self is lost; while alone, an individual is compelled to be what he is. There is no escape from the fact that truth relates to the individual. It is to the individual that philosophy looks for answers to its questions.

The conception that "existence precedes essence" is often cited as a defining feature of Existentialism. This formula is spelled out in a short essay by Jean-Paul Sartre.[4] In spite of the fact that Sartre has since disavowed some of his arguments in that essay, it does offer a picture of what is meant by "existential." While the definition is not developed in the same way by others, and would be criticized in particular by some of the religiously oriented Existentialists, it isolates certain factors with which most of the thinkers would agree.

Both "essence" and "existence" are terms with a long philosophical history. "Essence" has been used primarily to characterize those features of a thing that are permanently necessary to its being. If the features are absent, the thing cannot be. Traditionally, the notion of an essence of a thing was held to be prior in both being and importance to the particular existence of that thing. For example, the essence of a bed is outside of time. It is impervious to change, permanent, and that by which one defines a bed. In order for a carpenter to make a bed, he must have an idea of the essence of that bed. For a thing to have an essence, the essence must be in the mind of someone before the thing exists. The essence is thus "prior" to the concrete presentation of the thing.

In the world of objects, the essence of a thing often has to be prior to its existence. But the world of human subjects is different. Man is the only being who has the intelligence to conceive of an essence. Yet for the essence of a man to be prior to his existence, man would have to pre-exist himself, which is impossible. A man can only form the idea of his essence after he exists. He pre-exists any consciousness he has of himself. When he does define himself, he alone is responsible for the essence that he attributes to himself. He fashions his own image and has no permanent nature. He has only the condition that he creates. Thus, for man, existence is prior to essence.

Spelled out concretely, the priority of existence to essence indicates an interest in present situations, not in permanent ideals or fixed definitions. It moves human concerns away from absolutes and closer to particulars. For example, in a study of the mind-body problem, the Existentialist avoids the use of abstractions and tries to deal concretely with the ways in which the body and the mind are personally experienced and understood. Or in dealing with time, the Existentialist might argue that man's existence in time conditions the way in which he relates to time. Abstract time, or abstract space, is of little concern to him. Specific human relations move into the foreground, and the more general categories of logic and metaphysics are useful only insofar as they lead to an understanding of existential phenomena.

This suggests another feature common to the thought of the Existentialists. This is their lack of concern with logic and the philosophy of science. Of the five writers under consideration, only Jaspers gives extensive attention to science, and this is largely in relation to his work in psychopathology. Some of the Existentialists argue that science and technology go hand in hand, and that as a result, science is associated with superficial ideas of progress. Logic, a dry "technical" discipline, is ignored almost completely. Since many of the ideas of the Existentialists are ambiguous, or bordering on "mystery," the area in which logic can function is limited.

The common features of the Existentialist movement are to be found primarily within the philosophies—within the questions asked and the answers provided. An outstanding concern relates to the nature and function of philosophy itself. Dissatisfaction with the inherited conception of philosophy, along with a growing interest in philosophical method, is one of the major areas of inquiry shared by the movement as a whole.

A Conception of Philosophy

"The present writer is nothing of a philosopher." This statement echoes through Kierkegaard's preface to *Fear and Trembling*.[5] Though the exact identity of the "present writer" in this comment is obscure, there is little doubt that Kierkegaard is speaking in part for himself. His discomfort with contemporary modes of philosophy leads him to dissociate himself from the standard philosophical enterprise. If philosophy is what it seems to be in the present age, then he wants no part of it.

Kierkegaard is not the only Existentialist to divorce himself from the traditional conception of philosophy. His successors follow suit. Although they were educated in the thought and language of eighteenth and nineteenth century German Idealism, they reacted strongly against the philosophies of Kant and Hegel. Hegel, notably, was subjected to their attack. The "System," as Kierkegaard calls Hegel's philosophy, claimed to explain everything. His logic proposed that all thought, historical events, and natural phenomena went through common stages of development. In these stages, one could find a constant pattern with three components: a thesis, in which some phenomenon was posited; an antithesis, in which that phenomenon was denied; and a synthesis, in which the conflict between the thesis and the antithesis was resolved and transcended. Hegel used this pattern to organize all areas of human knowledge.

Most fervent in rebellion against this system is Kierkegaard. His attack focuses on the facile overcoming of contradiction. All conflicts were resolved by Hegelian thought; each conflict was mediated by the introduction of more inclusive categories. But Kierkegaard points out that such resolutions obscured the inevitable ambiguity, confusion, and incompleteness of human existence. He argues repeatedly that Hegel's enterprise was futile. Kierkegaard comments that

> in relation to their systems most systematizers are like a man who builds an enormous castle and lives in a shack close by; they do not live in their own enormous systematic buildings. But spiritually that is a decisive objection. Spiritually speaking, a man's thought must be the building in which he lives—otherwise everything is topsy-turvy.[6]

The castle of Hegelian Idealism, then, was a castle of sand. Because it was detached from the human beings whom it was built to house, it could not bring man closer to an understanding of his existence. Marcel points out, in describing the "sand castle" of Hegelian Idealism, that it alienated man from a sense of life as lived: ideas replaced individuals; the reality and destiny of the person were lost. Yet in spite of these criticisms, aspects of Hegel's method are incorporated into Existentialist thought. The phenomenological method and the conception of stages of human development can be found in the writings of all five of the philosophers under consideration.

It was not only Hegel's dialectical system that drew fire; other schools of Idealism also came under attack. In philosophy prior to Hegel, it is the implicit or explicit dualism to which the Existentialists object. From Descartes' mind-body dualism to Kant's separation of the noumena from the phenomena, philosophy has made a concerted effort to divide man from himself and from his world. But it is not just disillusion with Hegel's system or with dualistic philosophies that sparks the rejection of inherited conceptions of philosophy. The criticisms of Hegel are part of broader concerns. One common complaint is that philosophy has succumbed to the tendency to specialize. As it becomes an increasingly "technical" discipline, it moves into the rarified atmosphere of academic institutions. It loses its spirit of Socratic questioning and begins to pontificate. Philosophers are the only ones able to understand other philosophers, and what they attempt to understand is scarcely worth the time devoted to it. Broader questions are obscured in mazes of narrow, intricate "problems."

According to this critique, such specialization indicates fear in the face of the unknown. Confronted with a problem or question that is unanswerable, the technical philosopher will argue either that the problem is not philosophical at all or that is has been posed incorrectly. These arguments meet strong objections from the Existentialists. They counter with the claim that the fear of error and the avoidance of the· unanswerable question are violations of the very nature of philosophy. They argue for philosophical madness, not sanity, and for risk in dealing with the "large" questions, not for security. The unanswerable question is the very starting-point of philosophical concern.

The world of ideas, Kierkegaard declares, is sick. The symptoms of the illness are that ideas come too cheaply. When ideas are presented to make life easier and more relaxed, philosophy becomes fashionable but is no longer able to apply itself to its task. In trying to use the tools of philosophy to go beyond philosophy, its students have made philosophy an empty shell. "At every step philosophy sloughs a skin into which creep its worthless hangers-on."[7]

In particular, two forms of contemporary thought come under attack. These are Logical Positivism and Pragmatism. The criticism of Logical Positivism is part of the objection to increased specialization. When philosophy becomes concerned with the task of "methodizing and correcting" everyday reflections, its role is secondary. The important philosophical questions are sidestepped in the concern for increased scientific exactness. For example, the Logical Positivist would look at the fundamental question raised by Heidegger, "Why is there something rather than nothing?" and argue that it is a meaningless question. For the "scientific" philosopher, this kind of question should be cut out of philosophy. But the Existentialists would argue that such surgery destroys rather than heals. The questions tagged meaningless are in fact the *fundamental* questions.

The objections to Pragmatism are similar, in that it is argued that Pragmatism proposes too easy a way out of the difficult philosophical questions. Philosophy cannot always be directly learned or applied, as the Pragmatists claim. Nor does it always speak immediately to the present. The Pragmatists argue that the correct reasonings are those that have practical results, and as a consequence truth appears to be little more than practical success in dealing with one's world. One difficulty with Pragmatism is that it suggests that the object of philosophy is a *given*, much in the same way that one views the object of a scientific inquiry. But how can the object of philosophy be a given, the Existentialists ask, if we and our world are part of that object? Jaspers comments:

> Pragmatism seemed to be laying new foundations; but what it built thereon was nothing more than an aggregate of crude analysis of life and cheap optimism, was a mere expression of a blind confidence in the extant confusion.[8]

Common to the attacks directed against Logical Positivism and Pragmatism is a criticism of the adaptation of philosophy to science. With the growing predominance of science in Western thought comes a corresponding shrinking of philosophy. As the experimental method becomes more overpowering, philosophers feel that they must join the scientists and move with practical caution. As a result, the philosopher's appetite is diminished; he advances carefully through a world of resolvable problems. Ortega makes this point in *What Is Philosophy?*

> We need a complete perspective, with foreground and background, not a maimed and partial landscape, not a horizon from which the lure of the great distances has been cut away. . . . To assert that no manner of resolving the ultimate questions has yet been discovered is no valid excuse for a lack of sensitiveness toward them. All the more reason for feeling in the depths of our being their pressure and their hurt! Whose hunger has ever been stilled by knowing that he will not be able to eat?[9]

The criticisms of the Pragmatists are not reflected in the writings of all of the Existentialists, however. Marcel, for example, considers himself indebted to the work of both William James and Josiah Royce. The writings of the latter, whose Idealism was strongly tinged with Pragmatic ways of thinking, were instrumental in the development of Marcel's theories of intersubjectivity and participation. Also, James' work in psychology offers many examples of the use of the phenomenological method, which is endorsed by the Existentialists.

In the face of their objections to other views of philosophy, the Existentialists try to formulate a conception that escapes the traps of systematization, over-specialization, and practicality. They argue in common that philosophy must be redefined as a discipline. The redefinitions do not dissociate themselves altogether from past positions. The influence of Kant, as a result of late nineteenth century neo-Kantianism, is pervasive in the writings of Heidegger and Sartre. One also finds incorporated into Marcel's work many suggestions from the writings of Bergson, concerning both method and the nature of philosophy. But in spite of these influences, new directions are evident. Although the new definitions of philosophy are not all similar, they build on the same foundation. This foundation is the mutually recognized necessity for concreteness, personal applicability, and questioning in philosophy.

A variety of new conceptions appear. Philosophy is the spelling out of individual commitments. These commitments take their meaning from the fact that they are deeply experienced by the philosophers. In Kierkegaard's writings, this concern is evident. If his commitments have been experienced in the past, Kierkegaard uses a pseudonym. If they are experienced currently, Kierkegaard attaches his own name to his work. The meaning of ideas is forged as they find their way into his unique mode of existence.

In one sense, then, philosophy *is* a practical enterprise. As Jaspers points out, it is practical in that it grows from one's life and one's history.[10] This is not practicality *qua* utility or external applicability. It is the practicality of being engaged with human concerns. Philosophy asks a series of fundamental questions about man, communication, truth, and transcendence. Each question leads to another question, and the answer always carries the questioner a step further.

In addition, philosophy has its roots in the past. Heidegger develops this argument in detail. In uncovering the fundamental question, philosophy must inquire into the sense of being. This sense can only be revived by renewing a historical, spiritual vocation. A leap beyond ordinary questioning is necessary, but the very attitude of this leap is historical because it happens in time. In asking the fundamental question, man is called to encounter his past.

In the new conceptions of philosophy that are introduced, certain common features become evident. One is the view that philosophy cannot be carried on by a scholar at a respectable distance from his subject matter. He is engaged in this subject matter, whether he is willing or not. He is a part of what he describes and is the major source of the material he gleans on man's condition. Since it is *he* who is writing, his first questions must be those suggested by the fact that he is the person who raises the problems. In the face of this fact, man cannot help but participate in the philosophical project. He cannot separate himself from the philosophical enterprise. In no sense is philosophy an "objective" discipline in the way in which one might characterize science as objective.

Second, most of these thinkers seem to agree that philosophy is in some sense incomplete. The philosopher is *homo viator,* traveling in new directions, and never completing his journey. His work is not rounded out since as he drives towards the basic questions, he finds a number of them which do not permit final answers. In the course of breaking new paths, he threatens and upsets tradition. He challenges established values in the name of new perspectives. The objection to Hegel's system is implicit in this conception of philosophy, since the incompleteness of philosophy prohibits any final resolution of the problems raised.

It is only a short step to Heidegger's argument that philosophy makes things more difficult, not easier. Its task is to challenge what is the case, not necessarily to clarify it or to make it comprehensible. Thus it aims at jolting man's existence. The Socratic gadfly is very much in evidence. Just as the Athenian public was to be stung awake by Socrates, so contemporary man is to be warned into wakefulness by the "stormy petrels" of this new movement.[11] This object cannot be achieved by making philosophy a comfortable enterprise; it is achieved by making it difficult and disturbing.

It appears, then, that the Existentialists set themselves against the Western philosophical tradition in their understanding of the function and role of philosophy. The undercurrent of rebellion is strong. Kierkegaard's diatribes against Hegel leave little room for doubt as to the seriousness of his attack. Marcel's critique of functionalization and specialization in philosophy is developed in detail. However, any rebellion is rooted in the tradition against which it rebels. In setting themselves up against the Western view of philosophy, these thinkers indicate the force of this tradition and the influence that it exercises upon them.

Much of the material is new, but many of the insights ring of the past. Kierkegaard's conception of philosophy, for example, is strongly reminiscent of that of Plato. Like Plato, Kierkegaard emphasizes dialogue, allegory, and the physical setting of his philosophical works. For both Kierkegaard and Plato, philosophy is understood only if it is lived. Kierkegaard implies that if one has abandoned a philosophical position, he can only describe it by playing a role—the role of a person who is committed to that position. To experience fully a philosophical position or argument, alternative commitments must be transcended.

Nor is Kierkegaard alone in having his roots in the philosophical tradition he criticizes. That philosophy begins in wonder is affirmed by Marcel, but was said before by the Greeks. That philosophic thinking must begin anew is said by Jaspers, but was said before by Descartes. That philosophy develops in the context of history is said by Heidegger, but was argued before by Aristotle. It may be that the novelty in Existentialist conceptions of philosophy is located in the extremely personal dimension of these conceptions.

Philosophical Method

The uniqueness of the work of the Existentialists is also seen in their philosophical method. Related to any conception of philosophy is the question of how the philosopher plans to achieve his goal. If philosophy is the exploration of unanswerable questions, in what manner will this exploration take place? What tools will the philosopher use and what forms of reasoning? Or if philosophy involves the participation of the questioner in his subject matter, how will this participation be developed? For most of the Existentialists the question of method is inherited from Descartes and given impetus by the work of the German Phenomenologists.

A study of the methods used turns up a variety of them,

but with certain things in common. First there is a proliferation of styles and types of argumentation. Journal entries, lyrical "panegyrics," and allegories are used freely. This procedure is justified by the argument that ordinary philosophical methods cannot illumine the important questions. The Cartesian "clear and distinct ideas" or the Spinozistic propositions and corollaries are thought too regular and systematic. The verbiage and bulky apparatus of traditional philosophy are seen as so smothering the basic questions that these questions lose their force. The journal entries, dramatic and lyrical techniques, and short essays convey passion and commitment more readily.

The new ways of philosophic thinking provide an experiential picture of the important questions and answers. Perhaps this is one reason why so many of Sartre's philosophical ideas become strikingly vivid in his dramatic works. The ideas are sharpened and personified in the figures of his plays. And for Kierkegaard, many of the most forceful presentations are those worked out in lyrical or purely personal journal form. Because these ideas have emerged in a personal setting, they benefit from being communicated in terms of that same setting.

It can be argued that part of the approach of the Existentialists is the use of an unusual form of ostensive argument in introducing a point. In developing his notions of "dread" and "faith," Kierkegaard elicits the Old Testament figure of Abraham as an example of one who has these experiences. Direct philosophical prose is put to one side. One cannot make Abraham intelligible or his behavior orderly. The best that the philosopher can do is to batter away at the wall of unintelligibility. By looking at Abraham from different directions, one can reach towards the "boundary of the unknown land." Since this unknown land can never be completely explored, traditional philosophical language would be deceptive.

There is, as already pointed out, no one fixed method. Often one must follow a "winding path" whose outcome he does not clearly see. He may tell a story to make his point; he may develop an allegory; he may muse about his own experience. No material is excluded as possible philosophical content. The method is not fixed because the subject matter is not fixed. Marcel, for example, begins his philosophical output with a highly abstract *Metaphysical Journal,* in which he deals with problems raised by the German Idealists. Later in his work, however, he changes his approach and devotes himself to concrete, brief philosophical exercises.

Jaspers, Heidegger, and Sartre do not venture as far afield as Kierkegaard and Marcel in presenting their ideas. They often use the more traditional systematic methods of presentation, in spite of their rejection of the ideas of the philosophers who used these methods previously. The uniqueness of Heidegger and Sartre lies less in their style and mode of presentation than in their use of a specific kind of method—the phenomenological method.

The phenomenological method is primarily the product of the work of Edmund Husserl and his followers. Husserl maintains that philosophy can be a science. He does not try to argue that its content should imitate that of the specific sciences. He does suggest that its method must acquire sufficient rigor to carry philosophers to first principles, which would provide the foundations for all subsequent investigation. His project, reminiscent of that of Descartes, is to free philosophy of its undefended presuppositions—to find the most basic components of experience and the world. To arrive at a conception of consciousness and its objects that eliminates distorting presuppositions, he proposes a method whereby phenomena are grasped or "intuited." By particular analyses of phenomena, he hoped to eliminate all extraneous material and to discover things as they are—revealing the "essence" of the phenomenon but nothing peripheral to that essence.[12]

In different ways, some of the terminology, assumptions, and method of phenomenology are used by both Heidegger and Sartre. Sartre's subtitle of *Being and Nothingness* is *An Essay on Phenomenological Ontology.* Heidegger was Husserl's student and dedicated *Being and Time* to Husserl. The influence of Husserl on Heidegger becomes evident immediately in Heidegger's introduction to *Being and Time* where he says that the fundamental question of philosophy must be treated phe-nomenologically.[13]

However, there is no clear cut meaning of phenomenology which all of the Existentialists endorse. Often the most that one can say is that phenomenology is what each individual phi-losopher calls his method, even though these methods may have little in common. Whether Kierkegaard uses the phe-nomenological method can be debated, but his exploration of religious experience does seem to have some of the features of later phenomenological analyses. It is also the case that Jaspers does not endorse the phenomenological method di-rectly. Jaspers puts the method to use in his work in psycho-pathology in order to deal with pathological experiences but rejects the notion that philosophy is a science in the sense that Husserl's phenomenology would have it.[14]

Marcel occasionally claims that he does phenomenological analyses, but he does not do so in the strict sense that Hus-serl assigns to these analyses. Marcel's method is often a com-bination of critical studies and highly metaphorical evocations of personal experience. Marcel comments that what he means by "phenomenological" is the primacy of experience over pure thought.[15] An essay which he entitles "Outlines of a Phenomenology of Having" is a concretely based exploration into such experiential phenomena as possession, the experi-ence of the body, autonomy, and evil. For Marcel, phenome-nological analyses seem to be analyses of phenomena as they are directly experienced.

It is to Heidegger and Sartre that one must turn for the most complete statement of what the Existentialists mean by phenomenological method. For Heidegger, phenomenology is distinctly a method and does not include content. It is not the *what* of subject matter but the *how* of research. As a means of uncovering the meaning of being, it pushes beyond what directly shows itself. It is both the drive "to the things themselves" and a way of dealing with these things:

> It is opposed to all free-floating constructions and accidental findings; it is opposed to taking over any conceptions which

only seem to have been demonstrated; it is opposed to those pseudo-questions which parade themselves as 'problems,' often for generations at a time.[16]

Heidegger comments that philosophy is "universal phenomenological ontology," in that it deals with the way in which being manifests itself to human experience.[17] The phenomenon is that which can be brought forth by an encounter with it. The thing encountered is the phenomenon, although occasionally the phenomenon is disguised or hidden. Thus, phenomenology may include getting behind what conceals the phenomenon. Repeatedly in his studies of concrete experiences Heidegger moves through layers of material which he views as covering the nature of those experiences.

Sartre is indebted to Heidegger in that he uses phenomenology not as a systematic philosophical subject matter but solely as a method. It is a way of describing phenomena as they are met by human consciousness. Sartre does not develop detailed methodological discussions but seems to h ld with Heidegger that it is through an examination of consciousness and a revelation of behavior that one is able to develop meaningful discussion of man. For Sartre, for example, in a study of temporality, phenomenological description is a "provisional work whose goal is only to enable us to attain an intuition of temporality as a whole."[18] This description is pre-ontological, not ontological as Heidegger claims it is. It is an analysis of the "secondary structures" of temporality before working into a discussion of temporality as a whole. Phenomenology, for Sartre, is designed to clear the way for subsequent analyses that are not primarily phenomenological in nature.

In general, phenomenology as used by the Existentialists is not the specialized operations defined by Husserl's school. Nor is it a common set of rules. It is only a way of dealing with what presents itself to human experience. Its distinctiveness lies in the fact that it tries to avoid the superimposition of categories or directions upon that which offers itself to consciousness. As far as possible the presentation, or the phenomenon, is seen as it is. This is not to say that the phenomenological method claims objectivity. The phenomenon is a presentation to a subjective consciousness. But it *is* to say that as few operations as possible are made on the phenomenon. If it presents itself as confused, it is confused; if it presents itself as ugly, it is ugly. One looks neither for the reason for the presentation nor for the uses to which it can be put.

One of the better ways of exploring phenomenology's meaning for the Existentialists is to examine their specific phenomenological analyses. Heidegger's discussion of "curiosity," Sartre's study of the "look," or Marcel's inquiry into "having" provide examples. In these cases the philosophers agree in their feeling that the phenomenological method aims at a presentation of experience without deception. The analyses vary considerably in scope, but they return frequently to their source—specific personal experience.

Summary

Throughout the diversity of method and content of these thinkers, there is at least one constant. This is the desire to rethink and reformulate traditional philosophical problems. But is such a reformulation necessary? Is yet another picture of human experience needed? The Existentialists run the danger of multiplying confusions in a discipline already plagued by conflicting claims and terminology. Perhaps, indeed, the supposed novelty is deceptive, and the new categories and analyses are little more than the old ones disguised.

An Existentialist response to these questions can be made by posing a question to the critics in return. Is there any time when one does *not* need to reformulate and rethink the old questions? Insofar as man's experiences change, the issues are written anew because they arise out of and relate to new experiences. The old categories, while illuminating, are not completely adequate. A philosopher of the twentieth century faces different demands from those faced by a philosopher in the Middle Ages or in the seventeenth century.

Even to modify or revise old solutions to philosophical

problems in the hope of salvaging them does violence to the present. Although parts of those solutions may turn out to be relevant to contemporary philosophy, one cannot begin with this assumption. When Sartre redefines freedom, for example, he is not merely changing the language used by his predecessors. Nor is he taking their views and tacking on a few additions. He offers a new definition, one which would be meaningful to a twentieth-century European. That definition is built out of Sartre's personal experiences and finds its setting in the historical context in which he writes.

This is not to argue that the life of the twentieth-century European philosopher is necessarily more complex or more interesting than that of prior thinkers. But it is to suggest that this life is different. Changes documented by art and literature need to be documented by philosophy as well. Without this awareness of change, philosophy loses touch with experience, thereby breaking contact with its primary subject matter. This sense of change does not automatically justify the label of "pessimistic" or "destructive" that is occasionally attached to Existentialist philosophies. Rebellion and novelty can be signs of a highly constructive enterprise. In fact, philosophy has at times in its history been the stronghold of rebellion. The sympathy of Existentialist thinkers for Socrates suggests the strength of their identification with his interpretation of philosophy.

It is the attempt to reformulate traditional philosophical problems that occupies the remainder of the discussion in this book. Because one emphasis will be continuity with the past as well as the break from it, the format of the discussion in the different areas takes approximately the following pattern: First, a statement of the traditional problems that are the stimulus for the new considerations offered; and second, a description of the manner in which the problems are restated by the Existentialists. Since the way in which questions are raised often indicates the direction the answers will take, the reformulation of the old questions by these philosophers is at the heart of their position. In indicating why they find it necessary to rewrite the questions, the objections that they have to the positions of their predecessors are also considered.

Finally, the new answers to these questions are discussed. Sometimes the new answers are generally agreed upon, particularly in certain areas of ontology and theory of knowledge. At other points, the answers are quite varied, as in the philosophy of religion and in social and political philosophy. Often the Existentialist approach to philosophy includes a breaking down of the conventional distinctions between philosophical fields. The boundaries between epistemology, metaphysics, and ethics are not always clearly maintained. Occasionally the material under discussion moves into psychology or the social sciences. In no way do the Existentialists consider themselves bound to traditional disciplinary barriers.

For similar reasons, attention is directed to the "ontological groundwork" or "ethical perspectives" but not to systematic metaphysics or ethics. Epistemological, axiological, and metaphysical concerns tend to merge. The divisions in Existentialist writings are not apt to follow any established philosophical lines. They are more likely to be divisions indicating the chronological development of the author's views or the internal development of the subject matter. This material will be presented for the most part independently of formal criticism of their positions. The final chapter indicates paths that criticism has taken and could take. The major concern of this study is to examine Existentialism as a philosophy—to see it in relation to its past and as proposal for the future.

2

The Ontological Groundwork

Introduction

In a philosophical movement that claims to be nonsystematic, there are no self-evident propositions with which to start inquiry. A comparison of the Existentialists' views of the fundamental questions of philosophy indicates some of their starting points. These questions and the attempts to answer them suggest what these thinkers understand to be the basic issues confronting the philosopher.

Kierkegaard offers a variety of formulations of the fundamental question. At one point in his writings he argues that the entire body of his work is directed towards the problem of becoming a Christian. In a broader context, the fundamental question for Kierkegaard is linked to the task of becoming an individual. He comments, "If I were to desire an inscription for my tombstone, I should desire none other than 'That Individual.' "[1] This suggests that he regards the issue of subjectivity to be the key philosophical concern. The problems in the history of philosophy that Kierkegaard takes most seriously are those concerning the subject of experience. Philosophy must focus on the existing individual and on individuality, experienced as "passionate inwardness."

At first it appears difficult to link Kierkegaard's conception of the fundamental issues of philosophy with those of the other thinkers. Heidegger, for example, argues in *An Introduction to Metaphysics* that the central philosophical question is the question, "Why are there essents rather than nothing?"[2] Why is there something rather than nothing at all? Other questions may come first in time, but this question stands first in importance. "Something" encompasses all that is; there is no more inclusive category. In addition, the "why" is a demand for the source or ground of all being. If one can discover the ground of all that is, philosophy's most basic demand will be met. It is a discovery that only philosophy can make, not science or religion.

This concern for a foundation for inquiry is also evident in Sartre's major work. Sartre poses a number of initial questions in *Being and Nothingness,* but they group themselves around one central issue. This is the question of what kinds of being there are and of what their import is for human existence. At the outset of *Being and Nothingness,* Sartre asks, "What is the synthetic relation which we call being-in-the-world? What must man and the world be in order for a relation between them to be possible?"[3] The answers to these questions lead Sartre into an analysis of human experience in order to understand the unique kind of being that man possesses.

Marcel poses his basic question also in terms of the reality of the human individual. He states in *Présence et immortalité,* "there is a sense in which it is true to say that the only metaphysical problem is: what am I?"[4] Marcel's answer to this question permeates all aspects of his work—his studies of self-knowledge, values, the nature of the self, and interpersonal relations. He suggests that an understanding of man works from the analysis of concrete situations—the meaning of the phrase, "I have a body," for example, or the meaning of a mother's hope for the return of her son.

Jaspers argues that there are five basic questions arising out of a set of questions posed by Kant. Jaspers asks: What is science; how is communication possible; what is truth; what is man; and what is transcendence? He considers some of these questions more directly philosophical than others. For example, the question about science is raised to dispel the idea that the issues of science are more significant than those of philosophy. Each of these questions, in fact, pushes on to the next, so that it is the question about transcendence that is most crucial. The philosopher's task is to seek out being and in so doing to discover himself. Man is understood only in terms of what is other than and different from himself. The philosopher's goal is to discover a whole, and he works persistently towards a transcendent concept that will unify his experience.

In their formulations of the basic questions, the Existentialists do not divorce themselves completely from their predecessors. The questions of man and his world, of the kinds of being, and of the development of the individual can be traced back to the early Greeks. Both Jaspers and Heidegger emphasize that their relation to their heritage is not solely negative. They consider the reformulation of philosophical issues part of an attempt to renew a tradition. Their fundamental questions incorporate historical origins but are not limited to those origins.

Is there any one way in which these questions can be classified? They are at once ethical, psychological, and metaphysical. However, they do have an ontological base in common. In the history of philosophy, ontology has often been considered a subfield within the broader field of metaphysics. Metaphysics has included questions about the real, the cosmos, and relations that obtain within the real. Ontology's concern has been with the more specialized questions concerning the nature of being. For the Existentialist, ontological concerns transcend the boundaries of traditional metaphysics. At some point in each of the fundamental questions, the issue of being is raised. It may be the being of the self, the being of the world, or transcendent being. Here Kierkegaard joins the others with his questions about subjectivity. He asks what it means for the individual to *be*. To say, however, that the fundamental question is the question of being is not to say that Existential approaches to this question are identical.

It only suggests that such philosophies begin with an ontological groundwork that contributes the foundations for the remainder of the analyses.

The ontologies they develop are not primarily systematic, although at times those of Heidegger and Sartre suggest older philosophical systems. For the most part the Existentialists offer concrete explorations of a variety of issues in their attempts to understand the nature of being. Ontology includes epistemological, ethical, and religious concerns. It does not provide dogma, largely because many of the traditional dogmatic tools are no longer accepted. Instead, ontology is proposed as a starting point only—as a foundation for inquiries into knowledge, values, and action.

The Question of Being

In Western philosophy, questions about being go back to the pre-Socratic philosophers. The Existentialists frequently refer to the Greeks; Heidegger, in particular, develops his ontology with considerable attention to Greek terminology and arguments. Whenever raised, the basic ontological question has a similar form. It is the question of what it means to say that a thing is. This may include the search for the causes of a thing's being or the attempt to understand why a thing is. What brings something into existence and what causes it to go out of existence? More concretely, when one says that a man, a table, and a star all have being, is the same thing meant? It is particularly this last question that is of interest to the Existentialists. What kinds of being are there, and how is the search for being related to the seeker's own being?

Ontological questions appear highly abstract for a group of thinkers who claim to stress the concrete and the individual. Yet the Existentialists find themselves more at home with ontology than with most other traditional philosophical categories. The titles of some of the basic writings by themselves suggest the importance of the question of being. The major work of Sartre is *Being and Nothingness;* of Heidegger, *Being and Time;* and of Marcel, *The Mystery of Being.* A comparison of these titles to those of the books of seventeenth and eighteenth century philosophers shows a shift in emphasis from knowledge to being.[5]

Although the Existentialists use the language of traditional ontology, the direction and emphasis of their inquiries differ in that being is understood in terms of concrete human existence. There is no attempt to separate the inquirer from the subject matter of the inquiry. As a result, ontology is radically transformed. The question of being is studied from a subjective vantage point, and the inquiry into being is part of the attempt to understand the self.

In contrast to philosophical tradition since Descartes the question of being is regarded as prior to the question of knowledge. It is argued that epistemological issues have been given undue priority. Theory of knowledge has taken over the job of ontology. There have been attempts to justify the emphasis on epistemology by arguing that man relates most significantly to his world by knowing it. For Berkeley, for example, what *is* cannot be distinguished from what *is known.* This position is one of the most persistent stumbling blocks to an ontology independent of epistemology.

In different ways, all of the Existentialists take issue with the emphasis on knowledge that they inherit from Descartes. Not only do they find fault with the dualisms that accompany recent theories of knowledge, but they also argue that it is a mistake to do epistemology before ontology. Certainly being is grasped by knowing, but this does not make knowledge prior in importance. Knowledge does not exist in a vacuum. While one cannot analyze being without discussing knowledge, it can be argued that being is experienced prior to reflection about it. Because man is a *being* who knows, he *is* before he thinks about his being. Man's quest for being is at the root of his desire to know. He encounters phenomena first, and only later does he set out to understand that encounter. Heidegger suggests that the individual starts in a state of being and as a result of this state then goes on to make an inquiry into being. This inquiry is a latecomer in that it presupposes a prior ontological state.

It is not only the stress on knowing that leads to the criticisms of former ontologies. There is also a dissatisfaction with absolute ontological categories. Heidegger promises a "destruction of the history of ontology," largely to undo some of the fixed preconceptions inherited from Descartes and Kant. He points out that an understanding of the history of ontology would not make present methods any stronger. A typical mistake is the common-sense notion that when one deals with being, his concern is with a substance independent of man. This mistake makes the human being extraneous, an unnecessary addendum, standing in the way of "real" being.

The attempt to place man in the center of the picture is one of the major departures from tradition made by the Existentialists. Their reasoning is that if man is the entity that makes the inquiry into being, he should be the first concern of the inquiry. In his essay "What is Metaphysics?" Heidegger comments that "every metaphysical question can only be put in such a way that the questioner as such is by his very questioning involved in the question."[6] Man cannot avoid implication in the question of being because he is the being that raises the question.

These new directions predominate in Existentialist ontology, but there are also continuities with the past. The search for being is the search for forms of unity and coherent relations in the world. Insofar as it is the seeking of order, it is at one with a perennial philosophical inquiry. The major difference lies in the fact that unity and order here entail the transcendence of some of the classic dualisms that have separated man from himself and from his world.

However, there is also a new emphasis in the work of the Existentialists. Traditionally, ontological questions were a subordinate set of problems within the broader field of metaphysics. Yet for some of the Existentialists, questions within ontology are the only significant metaphysical questions. While confusions in terminology abound, it can be argued that most of the basic metaphysical issues for the Existentialists are linked to the question of being.

Sartre, at the conclusion of *Being and Nothingness,* distinguishes between ontology and metaphysics and claims to be engaged in the former only. He argues that ontology describes the structures of being whereas metaphysics raises questions of origin and explanation. Metaphysics is related to ontology in the same way that history is related to sociology. Whereas ontology is descriptive, metaphysics asks *why* things are as they are. Sartre does not say that the question of the origin of being is an insignificant one; rather he claims that it is not strictly an ontological question. He suggests a number of metaphysical questions that could be explored, but he does not pursue them.

This distinction between metaphysics and ontology is not maintained by the other Existentialists, and for the purposes of the present study, the term "ontology" will be used to cover a number of the issues which Sartre would consider metaphysical. For example, Heidegger's fundamental question of metaphysics, "Why is there something rather than nothing?" will be considered an ontological question. Attempts both to describe and explain being will also be included in ontology.

The first question then is the question of being. Prior to knowing and valuing, the comprehension of the nature of being conditions all subsequent analyses. In particular, comprehension in the sciences presupposes an adequate ontology. The objects of science have ontological status, and without some grasp of that status, scientific investigation is sterile. Jaspers points out that as soon as the philosopher tries to correct scientific knowledge, he finds that he must also deal with communication. To get at communication he must turn to man and to an understanding of what being is in relation to man.

Ontology is significant because questions of being underlie all other major issues, and even more crucial, because man is a creature uniquely interested in his own being. In the attempt to understand himself, he is pushed to question the kind of being that he is. Although he has, perhaps, a nonreflective sense of this being for a while, he is soon driven to reflect on it. A number of preliminary questions emerge out of such reflection. First, is it even true that being exists? What kind of being exists? And what is the relation of being to nonbeing?

Regarding the question of whether being exists, one of the most extensive answers is offered by Sartre in the introduction to *Being and Nothingness.* His argument offers a specific example of the Existentialist type of reasoning. It also introduces a number of central themes of the movement. Sartre discusses why being is a major philosophical concern and why a study of "being in the world" leads the philosopher to deal with the being of the self. In an earlier period Kierkegaard also focused on the being of the self, but he came nowhere near justifying his position with Sartre's thoroughness.

Sartre's proof that being exists has some of the earmarks of a philosophical joke. He uses one of the most eminent of philosophical arguments and turns it on its head. This is the ontological proof that argues from a definition of God's essence to the fact of the existence of God. Sartre reverses the ontological proof and tries to show that one can begin with things in the world, phenomena such as desks and lakes, and argue from their existence to a being that transcends appearances. It is possible to work back through the everyday entities of experience to a conception of being that goes beyond phenomena—having thereby some of the traits of "essence."

Sartre starts his proof by examining a fundamental stance of the human being—being in the world. Man encounters a number of phenomena in his world, such as tables, rocks, and storms. What kind of existence do these phenomena have? Is their *being* exhausted by the fact that they are experienced? Things seem to have being in their own right whether a person happens to experience them or not. However, it is hard to prove that they exist independently; as a result, Berkeley's subjective idealism becomes quite convincing. Sartre argues, on the side of "common sense," that being is more than what appears. But can he answer Berkeley? Is it possible to prove that there is a being-in-itself beyond what appears?

One problem that emerges is the possibility that the being

that transcends appearances could be the being of the person who experiences the world. There is something more than experienced phenomena, but that thing could be the self. A person has to exist for things to appear to him. In fact, he has a unique kind of being. He is not just the self that knows and experiences; he also exists in his own right. He is a being that exists prior to reflection. Sartre argues that man is conscious of himself even before he is conscious of an object. This self-awareness is immediate and nonobjective. For example, a man can look in the mirror and say "that's me." But in order for him to be able to say this, he must already be self-conscious before he reflects about it.

So at first, being is discovered in a somewhat unexpected place—not in the external world but in the self, the being that is a condition of knowledge and experience. But the search is not over. There is still the question of whether being exists in the world beyond appearances. What Sartre has discovered is the being that he calls "being-*for*-itself" and that others call the "subject," *Existenz,* or *Dasein.*

Sartre goes on to insist that there is being in the world as well—something that is more than what appears. He finds Berkeley wrong in the claim that the external world is equivalent to what is perceived. If objects in the world existed only because they were perceived, they would be totally passive and relative to the perceiver. Sartre denies that this is the case. Anything that is influenced by something else has active features. A hoe, for example, is not passive. A hand is able to wield the hoe because the hoe resists pressure put upon it. If the hoe did not resist, there would be no interaction; it would not function as a tool. In resisting, it shows itself to be active, not merely passive and inert. Similarly, the object of knowledge is not passive. It resists knowing in the same way that the hoe resists the hand. If it did not function actively, there would be nothing for the subject to know.

Nor is the object of knowledge totally relative to the subject. I know that there is a mountain twenty miles away from me. But it is not relative to my perception of it. If I were to say that the mountain is relative to me, I still would be referring to that which is independent of my perception. The fact of relation implies something that must be related. That of which I am conscious has an objective side to it. It is not solely what I make of it. There must be something on which consciousness works.

That being that is not passive and not relative to the observer is what Sartre calls "being-*in*-itself." It is active and objective—a being that is more than what appears but that is not the being of the self. It is difficult to characterize being-in-itself. Sartre suggests that it is revealed by experiences such as boredom and nausea. Being goes beyond what appears, but it is not a hidden quality of the object. It is "within" the object and yet it transcends the appearances of the object.[7]

Sartre's ontological proof, then, argues from the existence of appearances and the self to a transphenomenal being with two aspects. One of these aspects is the pre-reflective being of the self, and the other is the being-in-itself that transcends that which appears in the world. Being exists as a necessary condition of the experience of existing in the world. Sartre's position on this issue is one of the major Existential attempts to prove that being exists. Marcel, Kierkegaard, and Jaspers make no such extensive attempt. They assume that being exists and prefer to explore the ramifications of that assumption.

Sartre's conclusions indicate two aspects of being—the being of the self and the being of the external world. This polarity is accepted by all of the Existentialists. On the one hand the philosopher seeks to understand the self. On the other hand he investigates the transcendent being that goes beyond appearances. The second aspect of being is more difficult to explore; it is not disclosed by knowing and often there is only an intuitive comprehension of it. It is the first aspect of being that attracts greater attention from the Existentialists.

The Existentialists also find a close relationship between questions of being and nonbeing. Again the origin of the problem can be found in the writings of the Greeks. In dealing with being, one is confronted with nonbeing. It is difficult to think about being-in-itself without wondering what it is not. For being to have meaning, nonbeing must have meaning as well. In Heidegger and Sartre in particular, this concern is taken seriously. Heidegger points out that any question about being is also a negative question about nonbeing. Although Sartre differs with Heidegger about the question of the origin of negation, they both start by raising the issue of the meaning and importance of nonbeing. The first question is that of why one should take nonbeing seriously at all. It is a concept that is logically offensive. In speaking of nothing, one immediately makes it into something, thus presenting a contradiction. A set of meaningless propositions is introduced. In addition, there is something morally unsatisfactory about anyone who seriously allies himself with nonbeing. He becomes the prophet of disintegration, undermining civilization and looking at the dark side of things. In fact, Sartre, in *Existentialism Is a Humanism,* feels obliged to defend his philosophy against this accusation of pessimism and negativity.

These charges are met by the argument that the logic of the matter is not primary. Logic is not the ultimate court of appeal. Since the fundamental questions are ontological, logic takes a second place. Logic is meaningful only after one has a satisfactory ontology, not before. It is necessary to understand what is, before rules are introduced to explain or order it. There are ways of speaking about nonbeing that come out of authentic experience. Nonbeing is not created by being but rather by an encounter with being. Anything that a person confronts can always not be. For example, every man confronts the possibility of his own death. He can try to ignore it, but it is always there—nonbeing threatening to engulf his being. Also, all humans are faced with the fact that they are not what they might have been. In respect to those possibilities, each person may be said to be nothing. One may say of himself that he could have been a great skier or a superior student. But, in fact, he is neither. The being that he is wavers between something positive and something negative. In addition, what one is, one might not have been. Man resists the possibility of nonbeing just as he resists the possibility of suicide, but the possibility is always there.

Because of the pervasive presence of nonbeing, no one has

complete control over what he is. Heidegger points out that there is nothing to which man belongs entirely, not even himself. He can never compensate for all of the lacks within himself. In fact, just by raising the question of being, he indicates that "being" is something different from himself. Consequently he embodies a negation. Many different negativities appear in man's experience—in his need to question, in his expectations, in the fact that his possibilities are awaited but never achieved. As soon as the possibility of being something appears, the possibility of nonbeing follows. Man builds protective barriers but constantly faces the threat of being engulfed. He seeks being under the persistent pressure of nonbeing.

It is this ever-present threat of nonbeing that suggests why the quest for being takes on such urgency for some of the Existentialists. It also points out why there is more emphasis on the being of the self than on the being of the external world. Sartre, for example, starts by dealing with being-in-itself but moves almost immediately to a discussion of being-for-itself, or human reality. The quest for being becomes the quest for the being of the self. As man seeks being-in-itself, he immediately faces himself as a seeker. Although he starts with the intention of understanding being-in-itself, he finds that he turns back towards himself in an attempt to ward off the anguish of nonbeing and to discover and protect his own being.

The Search for Being

What is this being that man seeks? Most of the Existentialists start with the two kinds of being—being that is independent of the self and the being of the self. In *Truth and Symbol,* Jaspers speaks of the former as "the absolute, the all-causing, the unqualified" and suggests that the philosopher can take hold of it through the use of symbol.[8] Sartre considers it opaque and massive—that which is solid and self-identical. It cannot be described, for a description would link it to something that it is not. It fully, positively is, beyond negation and affirmation, beyond passivity and activity. The discussions of being occasionally move into the realm of religious experience, particularly in the writings of Marcel and Jaspers. But the foremost concern is usually the being of man.

While emphasis varies, most discussions suggest three loosely drawn stages in the quest for being. First, there is a recognition of a lack of being. Then, following the recognition of this lack, there is a drive towards being. Finally, there is a realization of being, or selfhood. It is on this third level that there is the most disagreement, since some claim that the self's being can never be fully realized.

It has been pointed out that ontology is accompanied by questions concerning the nature of nonbeing. If a phenomenon *is* one thing, it is *not* innumerable other things. One area in which this lack of being is exemplified is in the human subject. Experiences of human lack of being provide material for a number of concrete phenomenological analyses. The lack of being is the stage in which the self falls short. Man is shipwrecked on the reef of ontological lack. The deficiency of being is recognized as nothingness and is met with anguish and despair. Heidegger, for example, asks in *An Introduction to Metaphysics:* "How does it stand with being?" His answer is that man has lost his sense of being. In fact the question has little force because there does not seem to be any real issue about being or its lack. Since man has fallen short of grasping it, being has become unreal. Because it is impossible to see, hear, or touch being, the present age ignores it. Heidegger finds the refusal to encounter the lack of being the most direct indication of the lack.

To "fall out of being" means different things. Heidegger interprets it as a historical fact in the Western world, exemplified by a mass communication that has become a lack of communication. The sense of spiritual decline is indicated by the hatred and suspicion of anything free and creative. Marcel and Jaspers agree with Heidegger, adding as well that the question of being is meaningless because of a weakening of language. The fact that language is worn out indicates the destruction of a relationship to being. When language becomes a matter of mere messages, it moves steadily away from depth in experience.

In *Being and Having* Marcel pursues a dialectical approach to the lack of being. Ontological lack is manifested in functionalization and depersonalization. Men operate as machines, dehumanized in a mechanized world. The lack of being is characterized by a "having" orientation. Typical of this orientation are attempts to limit, define, and intellectualize the world. What one *has* is external to the *haver*. When possession predominates, things become primary and objects tyrannize over men. The experience of having, moreover, is not a stable one; it grows like a cancer. As soon as a thing becomes a possession, one tries to make it a part of himself in order to keep it from escaping and having a life of its own. But the possession is only a thing—a thing that can be lost or destroyed. Fears and anxieties hover around it. Each man hangs on desperately to what he has in the fear that it might be lost. Yet the harder he tries to hold onto it, the more it slips from his grasp. Eventually by a paradoxical reversal, the possession comes to control its owner. His life is turned into a slavery in which the master is possessed by his possession, the former slave.[9]

The lack of being is also felt in a weakening of communication. Contemporary man knows togetherness but not community, and togetherness only isolates him from his fellows. Kierkegaard pictures this lack of being as the inability to experience faith: many individuals exist in an aesthetic stage, in which life is only a series of idle moments. There is little consistency and no sense of duty. The predominant temperament is romantic, associating suffering with pleasure and living for the beautiful moment. Underlying principles are irrelevant to the aesthetic life. But even when principles and universals are introduced, a life can fall short of realization. One may then move to an ethical stage, in which duty is recognized and all standards are set by a group or class. Clarity is sought at the expense of individuality and people know little of striving. Man is unable to stand alone and therefore cannot realize his being.

Sartre's conception of lack of being is different from any discussed thus far, largely because he does not think that this state can be transcended. The self seeks being, but the quest is always frustrated. Man tries to close the gap between himself and his possibilities. He would like to be opaque and unified being-in-itself. If he could achieve this state, there would be no gap between himself and his values. He would not have to worry about his freedom or his responsibilities. Sartre characterizes this lack of being as the inability to be God. To be God would be to combine both the human and nonhuman aspects of being. One could have all the massiveness of being-in-itself, and yet the consciousness, possibilities, and creativity of the self. But man cannot be God, and his goal becomes a "useless passion." He is left with his desires and his freedom. God becomes the symbol of an unachievable goal.

The lack of being, then, means a number of things. It can be a lack of subjectivity, deficiencies in communication, or the inability to achieve a godlike completion. Combined with the lack is an experience of unlocalized anguish, which may not even be acknowledged. One sign of the lack is the functionalization and dehumanization of man. Deterioration of language reflects a loss of being, and neurosis and psychosis are its manifestations.

The new ontology, however, does not stop with a characterization of man's lack of being. There is a deep interest in the emergent recognition of the lack and in the ways in which it can be transcended towards a fullness of being. Both Heidegger and Marcel argue that there is an exigency or an appeal to the self from the self. If unrecognized, it is experienced as frustration; but if recognized, it initiates a movement towards self-realization. This is a call from the deepest level of the self—a call for a transcendence of the masks or pseudo-selves that have developed. It can be understood as a call of conscience or as the appeal of possibilities that the individual himself has formulated.

Heidegger stresses another level of this exigency in *An Introduction to Metaphysics*. This is a call to being that involves the renewing of man's historical existence. An individual's being is national as well as personal, and self-realization includes the fulfillment of a historical vocation. Not only is one called to be a complete person; he is also called to a creative fulfillment of his past and tradition. The source of this appeal is the heritage of which one is a part, just as the source of the appeal to selfhood is the self that one most fundamentally is.

There is, then, a drive to transcend the state of ontological lack. This is a call for the realization of the self and an abandonment of egoism and functionalization. It can be experienced, for example, in a situation in which one feels that his vocation is wrong for him. He senses that there is some other position in which he would be more fully himself. This experience leads to dissatisfaction with his state and the exploration of alternatives. If a satisfactory alternative is found, it can be said that he is more fully himself. He has come into a more complete command of the being that he is.

Another way of looking at this same experience is to say that a degree of inwardness has been achieved in which a man is no longer alienated from himself. This is not to say that all striving disappears. But it does suggest a change in the nature of dissatisfaction. When a lack of being is experienced, one is isolated from himself and the world. He then pushes towards a horizon that he never reaches. He experiences a constant unrest, giving urgency to the appeal of transcendence. As the self is realized, unrest may still be present but its character is different. There is a recognition that one is the very horizon that always seems to be in the distance. The horizon is the self that one might be—the complete and sufficient self.

As the individual moves closer to self-realization, there is a change that Marcel describes as a shift from a having orientation to a being orientation. The individual moves away from the anxieties and slavery of having. This shift occurs when one is "bound up with something serving as the immediate subject matter of a personal creative act."[10] In pure creation, the duality of the possessor and possessed is lost in a living reality. Marcel uses a distinction between a problem and a mystery to characterize the being orientation. A problem is a question posed. It subjects itself to analysis and division. A mystery on the other hand is a problem that encroaches upon its own data and invades them. It then is transcended as a problem. For example, evil is a mystery, as is death. These are not problems because one cannot stand outside of them and observe them. Death and evil are suffered; one's whole being is involved. The data of death are invaded, encroached upon by the fact of mortality. There is a direct personal investment in the issue. The concern of self-realization also is a mystery because one is the very subject matter being considered. In the being orientation, the person has no sense of his life as separate or as something he runs. He enters activities with the whole of his being, and he moves into a sphere beyond possession.

In spite of the fact that it is often necessary to talk obliquely about being, it is evident then that the Existentialists do find a series of stages in man's development that embody the search for being. These stages are not defined too closely, nor are they necessarily experienced in any fixed order. For Sartre, one of the stages is impossible of realization—that of the complete fulfillment of the self. And while the others do not exclude the possibility of ultimate self-realization, they suggest that it is a stage that is seldom achieved. Most people become fixed in various situations of ontological lack, obscurely experiencing a call to being but unable to move beyond their present state.

It is evident that the proposed ontology is removed in many ways from traditional ontology. A significant difference is the close relationship between ontology and psychology. Because of the ties between the two disciplines, ethical questions are linked directly to ontological issues. What the individual is and what he should do cannot strictly be separated. While it may not be possible to derive a moral philosophy from an ontology, ontology serves as a springboard for ethics.

If there is a "destruction" of the ontological tradition by the Existentialists, it is primarily the destruction of a static conception of being. This destruction started with Hegel, and echoes of the Hegelian dialectic appear in all of the writings of the Existentialists. Being is dynamic; it is in time. There is a growth or development of being, evidenced specifically in the being of the self. This position alone undercuts much of the abstractness of ontology and makes concrete phenomenological analyses of human experience germane to ontology.

It was suggested at the beginning of this chapter that the Existentialists start with ontology because it is fundamental to the theory of knowledge. Without an ontology, knowledge is incomprehensible. Man's attempts to know are part of the quest for being, which is illustrated by the movement towards self-realization. It is through knowledge that the philosopher arrives at an understanding of that quest, but there must be material for knowledge to use. Once the outlines of an ontology are proposed, questions of knowledge follow immediately. A major path to being is through knowledge. An inadequate theory of knowledge veils being, whereas an adequate one reveals it. The Existentialists' extensive work in epistemology suggests that they find confusions about knowledge to be particularly damaging to philosophy. From questions of being to questions of knowledge is a short step. Through knowledge, being is organized and understood; but it must be organized in ways that do not distort it.

3

Theory of Knowledge: The Critique

Introduction

Theory of knowledge follows closely upon ontology. A principal approach to being is through knowledge, and a significant feature of man's being is his ability to know. Knowing is a major way of gaining access to the self, to the world, and to other people. Existentialist theories of knowledge can be considered from two directions: their criticisms of past epistemologies and their reformulations and solutions of the basic epistemological problems. The Existentialists take issue with both Rationalism and Empiricism and offer a number of proposals concerning how questions of knowledge should be raised and how the fundamental issues should be resolved.

All of them are influenced by Descartes, who posed the major epistemological issues for subsequent Western thought. There are three basic questions that can be used as aids in understanding theories of knowledge since Descartes. The first question concerns the knower. What is the entity that knows? Considered sometimes as the self, or more narrowly, the mind, the subject of knowledge was crucial to Rationalism but began to lose importance in the writings of the Empiricists. In Hume's *Treatise on Human Nature,* neither the mind nor the self were treated as meaningful ideas. Hume argued that no corresponding impressions for these conceptions could be found.

Other epistemological concerns are related to the above question of the knower. One is the problem of other minds. Does every mind think the same things? People often encounter the world in radically different ways. Furthermore, there is no guarantee that one person adequately communicates his ideas to another. This raises the question of whether it is ever possible to know what goes on in another's mind. An associated epistemological concern is that of self-knowledge. Although it is possible to speak of things in the world as objects of knowledge, there are philosophical difficulties in considering the self an object. The self would have to be both the knower and the thing known. A theory of mind or of the self must account somehow for knowledge of the self.

The problem of self-knowledge leads to the second major question in the theory of knowledge: What is it that is known? How does one describe the object of knowledge? It can be thought to be the facts—things independent of man; or it can be considered ideas, as Berkeley suggested. The question of the object of knowledge also brings up the issue of truth. When is it possible to say that one makes a true statement? Is truth the relation of ideas to something independent?

Problems concerning truth lead to the third question. In considering the connection between man's ideas and the world, one moves to the issue of the relationship between the knower and the known. It is in this third area that issues of perception and reason appear. Knowledge involves perception, sensation, reason, and memory. Do these different modes of encounter yield information about the world as it is, or is some process of interpretation necessary? In addition, there is the question of whether the way one understands the world distorts it. Is the world exactly as it is encountered, or does the mind filter its material?

A look at two typical answers to these questions will set the stage for the Existentialist critique. A Rationalist would argue that the entity which knows is mind, a substance. Man is, by definition, a rational animal. It is his reason alone that distinguishes him from other animals. This unique faculty sets him aside and allows him to draw inferences. That which he knows is the external world, and knowledge reveals the world as it is. For the Rationalist, ideas copy or represent the world, and he conceives of the relationship of his mind to the world as implemented primarily by reason. Perception is necessary for the initial encounter, but it is corrected by reason. Truth about the world has to do with the way ideas relate to each other. The orderliness of ideas indicates the orderliness of the world, and communication is carried on by a mutual interpretation of ideas.

An Empiricist might accept the view that the mind is what knows, but he does not accept so readily a substantial conception of the self. He assumes the fact of knowledge and spends more time on the question of what is known than on that of the knower. One knows ideas or groups of ideas. Reason may eventually work on perception, but the starting point is the ideas provided by sensation and memory. They are the building blocks on which complex thoughts are based. Some Empiricists claim that ideas represent an independent material world; others deny this. A fairly typical position would be that ideas may represent an external world but that it is impossible to determine what that world is really like. The only access to the world is through sense impressions.

Of particular interest to the Existentialists are the dualisms that stem from traditional answers to the three questions. Most prominent is the mind-body dualism, a position that recent epistemologies inherit from Descartes. The dualist argues that the mind and body are separate. The mind is that which is uniquely human, and the body belongs to the external world of objects. A second dualism is the separation of appearance and reality. That which appears is given in sense perception. Because appearances are often deceptive, the philosopher's task is to look for reality behind the appearance. Reality is permanent, unchanging, and stable, whereas appearances are in flux.

Finally, there is the subject-object dualism. Both Rationalists and Empiricists argue that there are two entities in the knowing process, the subject that knows and the object that is known. They are separate but must be related for there to be knowledge. With this dualism, as well as the others, the problem is to unite the two poles. It is easier to split up the components of knowledge than it is to unify them into a coherent picture of human activity. It is on this issue that a number of the Existentialists begin their criticisms of traditional epistemologies.

The Existentialists, while criticizing much of classic epistemology, are still indebted to the work of earlier epistemologists, particularly to Descartes and Kant. Jaspers takes his fundamental questions directly from questions posed by Kant. Heidegger, who wrote two books on Kant, planned a major part of his work to deal with the problems posed by Descartes and Kant. Both Kierkegaard and Marcel discuss Kant in detail, and Sartre introduces *Being and Nothingness* with a discussion of Cartesian and Empiricist theories of knowledge.

To understand the new directions proposed for the theory of knowledge, it is important to see why there is dissatisfaction with the inherited conceptions. The rejection of traditional viewpoints is based first of all on a criticism of the ways in which epistemological questions are posed. The type of questions asked in any philosophical field limit the kind of answers that can be given. Thus the criticisms of traditional epistemologies first consider the manner of raising questions about knowledge.

The Criticisms

The three basic epistemological questions are: What is the knower?; What is the known?; and What is the relationship between the knower and the known? The presuppositions behind these questions and the way in which they are posed already limit the answers that can be given. The questions suggest that one can radically separate the knower from the known. This implies that knowledge can be split and that it is possible to deal separately with the subject and object of knowledge. In raising the issue of the relationship between the knower and the known, the third question implies that the philosopher has taken two things apart and will try to put them back together. The assumptions of dualism are already present, even before the analysis of knowledge is underway.

The difficulties that Existentialists have with the epistemological tradition crystallize in the reactions to Descartes. Marcel, for example, objects to Descartes' *cogito ergo sum,* because it dealt with the self as a thinking being only. It neglected other aspects of human experience that were equally important, such as the existence of the body or the fact of action. Descartes separated the mind and the body, ignoring what Marcel considers to be an obvious unity. Also the Cartesian position isolated the self from other selves, underplaying the fact of intersubjectivity.

The attack on Descartes is even more explicit in the positions of Heidegger and Sartre. In his discussion of the world in *Being and Time,* Heidegger objects to the unjustified splits in Descartes' position. The "ego cogito" was separated from the "res corporea" without any analysis of the kind of being that these entities have. Heidegger finds that Descartes used the notion of material substance as an explanatory concept for the being of the world. Yet substance was indefinable in the Cartesian position and was passed off as something incapable of clarification. Descartes never explored the being of the world. He used a mathematical model but did not explain how he arrived at this as a satisfactory means of understanding the world. The general criticism that Heidegger makes is that Descartes worked from traditional methods and as a result did not resolve the problem of the self and its relationship to the world.

Another criticism of Descartes can be found in Sartre's introduction to *Being and Nothingness.* In trying to clarify knowledge, Descartes separated appearances from something real behind the appearances. There was a split of the exterior and the interior, with essence standing behind the appearances and supporting them. Sartre finds no evidence for the existence of privileged natures hidden behind phenomena. Why should the appearance of a chair be unreal? In this respect, at least, Berkeley was right. The appearance *is* real. The chair that appears is the real chair. Essence is only the principle that groups together a series of appearances. Sartre goes on to point out that while things appear in two modes, they are two aspects only, not two different kinds of substances. These two poles are both appearances. Sartre does say that certain dualisms are necessary, because man needs to differentiate between the self and the world. In addition, the self is an important starting point of inquiry. But it is part of the whole relationship of being in the world. Consciousness is never separate from that of which it is conscious. It does not exist alone in solitary Cartesian grandeur.

The attacks that Marcel, Heidegger, and Sartre direct against Descartes emphasize a common antagonism to dualism. The self is a whole existing in a world; it cannot be divided up without distortion. To say that there is a world completely separate from the self is to sidestep the question of the nature of the world. If the reasoning self is established as a privileged substance in the world, the whole question of consciousness and knowledge is obscured. The mind that knows, the world that is known, and the relationship between them cannot be separate issues.

A major area in which the Existentialists take issue with their predecessors is thus the reliance on the subject-object distinction. Kierkegaard was the first to find this polarity unsatisfactory. His repeated call for subjectivity is a reaction against attempts to find truth in the object. To say that reality resides in an object that is grasped by a subject is to isolate the individual from reality. Instead of clarifying knowledge, this makes it impossible. By considering truth objective, man converts truth to untruth. One may think, for example, that the truth about a great symphony lies in the object—that is, in the score, the instruments, or the structure of the movements. But this is to build barriers between oneself and the music. In the course of an objective analysis, the symphony is lost.

Kierkegaard's concern in attacking the subject-object relationship is not primarily epistemological. But in the writings of the later thinkers, the criticisms are focused specifically on questions of knowledge. Jaspers, for example, in *Truth and*

Symbol, points out that the subject and object in past epistemologies are each raised to absolutes. Then, either one or the
other is unduly stressed. In particular, the object is over-
emphasized, and there is an insistence on an objective reality.
Man is told to take account of objective reality first, before
concerning himself with his reactions or feelings. Jaspers argues
that this attitude conceals being instead of revealing it.

In Heidegger's *Discourse On Thinking,* a similar point is made.
He criticizes the view that thought is the representation of
a phenomenon. The problem with this approach is that
thought, so conceived, converts its object into a fixed thing.
But the object is not fixed. As soon as one represents to himself what he is waiting for when he thinks, he no longer waits.
The subject-object relation is an unfortunate historical varia-
tion of the relation of man to the thing. It turns man into a
subject before he has time to be a man, and it converts things
into objects before they have time to establish themselves as
things. If man is equated with an ego-subject, he is unable
to understand himself.

One of the more interesting analyses of the subject-object
distinction does not come from any of the main figures under
consideration here, but it is relevant to the discussion. This
is the study of the I-It relationship, developed by Martin
Buber in *I and Thou.* He characterizes the I-It or subject-
object relationship as an attempt to mend a break between
a subject and a thing. The subject conditions itself to treat
a thing objectively, by seeing it as a picture or as a fixed
quantity. To remain on this level of being is to lose some of
the more important meanings of experience. The thing is a
bundle of qualities and is dealt with solely as something past.
When objectified, it has no present meaning.

A major source of dissatisfaction with the subject-object
relationship is with the hardening and distorting of experience that results from the distinction. It isolates things from
their settings, forcing them to be observed as if from a distance. By relying heavily on the subject-object relationship,
man becomes a spectator, staying carefully apart from the object that he observes. This suggests that the object of knowl-

edge is something one can dispose of. Since it is totally separate from the person who deals with it, it does not significantly influence this person. It is this gap that is so unsatisfactory to the Existentialists. How can one stay distant from what he knows, especially when the knowledge is supposedly his? The subject-object relationship is criticized, then, for not holding true to experience. Man experiences things in a unitary fashion—not in pieces. In knowing, he cannot readily separate himself from his body or his world. All three exist together.

Subject-object dualism also weakens the meaning of language. While it seems as though language is a source of this dualism, in that the subject-predicate distinction is central to propositional discourse, such an interpretation does not take account of the depths of language. Kierkegaard's use of language is based on the view that language is lived experience by which the most fundamental insights are expressed. It is not simply rules of grammar. Kierkegaard's pseudonyms suggest his unique view of words. His writings present an entire cast of characters. Kierkegaard's use of this method can be attributed to his notion that a philosophical position must be held with the philosopher's whole being. For example, an individual may be faced with the alternatives of being a believer or an atheist. His decision cannot be made by a cold study of the advantages of each position. If this method is pursued, the decision is unreal. He has not lived either alternative. Just to say that he is a believer or an atheist will not make him one. He must know internally the communion and immeasurable pull of faith in order to be a believer. Or he must experience to the full the sudden shock and freedom of atheism.

Heidegger deals directly with questions of language and also feels that grammatical rules exist on the surface of language only. To cite subject-predicate grammar in defense of the subject-object distinction is to miss the deeper meanings of language. Language directly reflects a state of being. If thinking is categorical or calculative, language will show an inability to meditate. Names do not designate things strictly;

words must be *heard.* Heidegger often turns to the Greeks for illustration of his point. He suggests that the Greek language actually brought things into being. It created concepts and articulated experience in words. The words then began to have a life of their own. The early words about being can lead back to the basic question about being, if one goes beyond the words to their meaning instead of stopping and asking what they represent. If allowed to, the *logos,* or the word, will indicate what experience is about and will allow things to be perceived.

In *Truth and Symbol,* Jaspers suggests that language is the tool that fulfills man's constant urge towards clarity. But the objectification of language, particularly by the use of philosophical categories or catchwords, obscures philosophy's origins. Metaphor and symbol often come closest to indicating the wonder out of which first questions are raised. In fact it is often the intuitions of poets that best unfold the experience of being, by use of symbolic discourse. A task of philosophy is to make the language of symbols clear. By meditation on the symbol, its meaning is deepened; and with the help of symbols, the philosopher can move through everyday empirical thought to a consciousness of being. But if objects are separated from subjects and if language is intended to indicate objects, there is no way of deepening experience through language.

Criticisms of traditional epistemological positions, then, first raise issues about the questions conventionally asked in the theory of knowledge. The Existentialists suggest that these questions are incorrectly posed and that they limit answers to a narrow objective sphere. The attack focuses in particular on Descartes, because his approach to the theory of knowledge set the stage for subsequent epistemologies. Criticism is directed more specifically against the subject-object split, which led to undue emphasis on the object. It allowed man to be defined as a rational, thinking being and then to be separated from his world. The hardening of language consolidated this split, and the subject-object and mind-body dualisms became incorporated into epistemology.

A final aspect of this critique of the subject-object distinction is the attack upon the overemphasis on the object in science and technology. Heidegger, in *Discourse On Thinking*, suggests that the prevailing object orientation allows man to flee from contemplative thinking. Technology kills meditation, and even history is converted into a science. Jaspers, a scientist himself, also has reservations about the use of science. One of his basic philosophical questions is the question of what science is, but he raises it partly to point out that this question should not be given undue emphasis over ontological questions. He argues that philosophy is not a science and cannot be objectified. Granted that science can incorporate man's wonder and desire to know and free him from limited dogmatic views of the world, it still is not the paradigm for all philosophy. It cannot embrace many of the broader questions. The knowledge of science is worthless if it cannot be communicated, and the question of how communication is possible leads to questions about man's being. The philosopher hopes for more than just correctness in science. The truth is not limited to that which is merely logically correct.

Man is approached from many sides by scientists. He is studied by psychologists, biologists, anthropologists, and sociologists. But these studies do not necessarily provide a sense of the whole. Sartre graphically illustrates this point in his discussion of the body in *Being and Nothingness*. When the body is defined scientifically as a thing with its own laws, that definition is hard to fit to one's own consciousness of his body. The body does not appear as an object in the midst of the world. Nor is it experienced as the thing on the operating table that the doctor classifies as an object. If objectified, all of its possibilities are turned into dead possibilities. Consciousness refuses to let itself be bound to this body-object. None of the Existentialists would propose to ignore science, but all argue that a scientific tendency to overemphasize the object increases the distortion of human experience. Most agree with Jaspers that science yields many beneficial effects. The danger comes when science reduces man. When he is characterized as a being that can be described objectively, aspects of his subjectivity are lost or go unnoticed. Consciousness and selfhood are ignored.

In the light of these criticisms the question emerges as to whether the Existentialists are themselves able to by-pass the basic categories of Western epistemology. How is it possible to deal with knowledge without asking questions about the knower, the known, and the relationship between them? They talk about the self, the world, truth, and perception. Are they in fact relying on the basic dualisms of past epistemologies in spite of their extensive criticisms? To deal with this question it is necessary to turn to the positive aspects of their epistemologies. The first step is to see how they raise epistemological questions. Since a major objection to their predecessors is that questions about knowledge are not adequately formulated, it is important to see how the Existentialists alter these questions and whether they avoid the problems that they find in the way questions are traditionally asked.

The Reformulations

The Existentialists' approach to epistemology can be traced in part to a specific conception of thinking and reflection. Heidegger's *Discourse On Thinking* proposes, for example, that philosophical thinking is meditative, not calculative. Calculative thinking catches man up in planning and classification. Heidegger comments that "the world now appears as an object open to the attacks of calculative thought, attacks that nothing is believed able any longer to resist. Nature becomes a gigantic gasoline station, an energy source for modern technology and industry."[1] Contemplative, meditative thinking, on the other hand, releases a person to himself. Heidegger frequently suggests that "waiting" is necessary. What one waits for is not something that can be strictly planned or calculated. In fact, if man knew what he was waiting for, the attitude would no longer be "waiting" in the sense that Heidegger gives it. This active waiting allows truth to be revealed. Reflection is the attempt to go towards the self by waiting for it. This conception of reflection is closely tied to the ontological position that man attains to his being—a being that is in fact already implicitly present.

Heidegger argues that in seeking an answer to the fundamental question of metaphysics, man *wills* to know. He gives the term "will," however, a special meaning. It refers to an attitude of utter commitment. An illustration of this attitude is Abraham's decision to sacrifice Isaac, as described by Kierkegaard in *Fear and Trembling*. Abraham wills to sacrifice Isaac and puts his whole existence at stake in this willing. A task is set, and the individual makes himself ready to accomplish it. Heidegger points out that there is "a leap through which man thrusts away all the previous security, whether real or imagined, of his life." [2] It is a privileged happening in intellectual life when the fundamental questions are really asked. Thinking is questioning, and questioning is a basic human force. But this is so only if man does not seek a calculated object.

For Heidegger, reflection is not the mere acquisition of information. It entails being *able* to learn. The person with information can still be perplexed when he encounters reality. He may be able to function successfully in the technological world, but in an ontological sense he may be a bungler. For example, extensive information about the world is of no help in the face of the death of a friend. Facts provide no handles with which to confront this reality. To know the meaning of the death of another, one must actually "stand in" that death. One only learns when he understands that he must learn again and again by living what he learns.

Reflection, then, is not passive. It requires the disciplining of an attitude. Kierkegaard sees this clearly. In a series of comments in *Fear and Trembling* he points out that Abraham retains Isaac only through a form of disciplined internal freedom. The father exhausts himself, risking all; as a result he regains his son. Kierkegaard could be describing philosophical reflection as well as religious faith. To achieve insight, one risks all that he has. This may entail breaking out of the great philosophical systems that seem so secure. Reflection is an awakening in which man sees how much he lacks, and in which he is aroused to new forms of inquiry and meditation.

For Jaspers, the discipline of meditative thinking is one that encompasses both subject and object and transcends them. It is a stage beyond empirical inquiry. The philosopher cannot ignore the world of everyday existence, but this world is not his central concern. On the level of empirical existence, each man appears to his fellows as a physical, psychological, and biological object. Philosophical reflection moves past this level, encircling all dualities. Reflection, for Jaspers, is a listening—a concept close in many ways to Heidegger's "waiting." The usual mode of cognition of objects is not satisfactory. Reflective listening allows the philosopher to move towards being, by the use of symbols.

Marcel suggests that the mode of reflection that the philosopher uses is secondary reflection, whereas knowledge on the subject-object level is primary reflection. Primary reflection breaks experience up into its component parts, and leads to Cartesian mind-body dualism. Secondary reflection, however, is recuperative in nature. It reconquers the unity of experience that is shattered by primary reflection. Only secondary reflection can do justice to the immediacy of experience. Primary reflection takes the object reflected upon and categorizes it, whereas secondary reflection permits an understanding of what a thing is in its own right.

Philosophical reflection, then, is a mode of contemplation. The paradigm for such reflection is contemplative self-encounter. This is not curiosity, nor is it concerned with locating the self in time. Unlike a spectator the philosopher participates in the reality he contemplates; he does not merely observe it. In this participatory experience, communication is primary, whether it is with others or with oneself. The nature of philosophical contemplation seems to be most fully realized in recollection, a form of turning inward in order to understand the self. Openness and availability are central to this kind of reflection, whereas rigid use of the will or critical resistance make it impossible.

The only position that at all shows itself at odds with this account is that of Sartre. The conception of participatory experience just described does not appear in Sartre, and there is reason to believe that he would consider such unified reflection impossible. However, there is a partial parallel in Sartre's distinction between pure and impure reflection. He introduces these conceptions in conjunction with an analysis of temporality. Pure reflection is the original form of reflection in which there is a simple presence of the self to the self. In the course of pure reflection, the three dimensions of time appear. There is an experience of the self as a being in the past, the present, and the future.

Impure reflection, however, seeks to determine the self; it is an abortive attempt to solidify the self into a thing. The self is posited as a transcendent object, and a series of psychic facts are introduced to explain it. Impure reflection produces psychological categories, such as the notion of the ego or the unconscious. Sartre's conception of impure reflection comes closest to what the other Existentialists refer to as objective or calculative thinking. It assigns a set of characteristics to the psyche and then tries to pull them together into a synthetic whole. The result is a pure multiplicity, which is in no way unified.

For Sartre, knowledge is one step beyond reflection. It is an immediate distinction that man makes between himself and his world. Things in the world are given a spatial dimension, and qualities and potentialities are ascribed to them. He does not suggest that the experience of the world must be participatory, but he does point out that neither the subject nor the object can be isolated and absolutized in the knowing relationship. Pure reflection, in his theory, has much in common with Marcel's secondary reflection and Heidegger's contemplation.

A major feature of the various conceptions of reflection is that they all reject any view that allows reflection to divide or split its object. Genuine philosophical reflection tries to get as close as possible to the synthetic wholes with which it deals. The first concern of reflection is to arrive at an adequate grasp of the self. This is not achieved by objectification but by a form of intuitive understanding. There is not universal agreement about the degree to which this understanding is possible, but all grant that it is possible to some extent. Philosophical reflection is not a planned encounter with an object but a recovery or discovery of being.

These views of reflection suggest why the Existentialists find themselves unable to use the format of traditional epistemologies. The questions raised by former theories of knowledge make calculative or objective thinking the goal rather than meditative reflection. For the Existentialists, therefore, epistemological questions must be posed differently—in a way that does not presuppose the subject-object distinction and that does not require dualistic or objective answers. Occasionally, they retain some of the old terminology, but it is used in new ways.

The epistemological questions that the Existentialists raise are posed whether answers are thought to be possible or not. In some cases an unequivocal answer may not even be expected. One reason for this is the recognition that the questioner is directly involved with the question he asks. He is part of its subject matter and characterizes his own experience when he answers the question. Thus no question can be answered objectively, nor can any answer be neatly completed or rounded out. The resolution of a problem grows with the experience of the philosopher.

Take, for example, one of the major epistemological issues, the issue of the self. The question is, "Who am I?" This is not a simple question. As Marcel points out, it is a problem that encroaches on its own data. The inquirer's existence "invades" the material under consideration. The identification of the self with mind only—a position stemming from Descartes—is accounted unacceptable. Rather, when one asks, "Who am I?" he is also asking about his body and his past. The question immediately raises the issues of temporality and mortality. The ability to know is only one feature of the self. Having, doing, and acting are equally important.

The self does not exist in isolation. It is in the world and with others. The question of what the object of knowledge is, is an attempt to understand the world and other people. But these issues cannot be seen merely as the problem of the external world and the problem of other minds. Instead of asking whether there is an external world, one asks how the experience of being in the world can be described. An understanding of being in the world in turn clarifies the meaning of truth. The shift in questions in this area indicates that the concern is with wholes, not with separate pieces.

Just as the self is in the world, it is also with others. This is not a question of whether one can know what goes on in the mind of another. Instead it is a matter of reflecting on the implications of being with others. Given the fact that man is enmeshed in intersubjectivity, what insights can be gained about relationships with others? To what extent does being with others in a world make a person what he is? In the relationships under consideration, man as a knowing being is not readily separable from man as an acting and valuing being. In the theory of knowledge, the questions of value and responsibility continually appear. To some extent, in doing epistemology, the Existentialist is also establishing a foundation for ethics.

The reformulated questions of the theory of knowledge can be summarized as the following. The question of what the knower is is converted to the question of the way in which the self exists in relation to its body and lives in time. It is the question, "Who am I?" The question of the object of knowledge is converted to the question of what it means to be in the world and with others. And the problem of the relationship between the subject and object of knowledge does not come up at all, since subject and object are not separated in the previous questions. The reformulations of the questions of knowledge suggest that knowledge has a much broader meaning for the Existentialists than for their predecessors. The inclusion of discussions of feeling, questions concerning the nature of the body, and a whole range of considerations about interpersonal relations and communication indicate that there is no strictly delimitable Existentialist epistemology. Questions of knowledge are inextricably tied to questions of being and value and involve issues of philosophical psychology and anthropology.

4

Theory of Knowledge: The Proposals

The Self and Self-Knowledge

The Existentialists refer to the self in many different ways. Heidegger's *Dasein* and Sartre's "for-itself" are the most well known. But one also finds Kierkegaard speaking of the "subject" and Jaspers of *Existenz*. All of these words refer to the self, and the variations in terminology indicate differences in emphasis only. Heidegger's word, for example, stresses man's "being-there," whereas Sartre's points to a fissure in human experience.

Even though Kierkegaard uses the word "subject," this is not a return to the subject-object distinction. Subjectivity is a value to be achieved, not a necessary condition of the knowledge of an object. It entails a commitment in which action is built on objectively uncertain premises. Socrates is one of Kierkegaard's examples of such commitment. In the discussions in the *Phaedo,* Socrates represented a concrete stance towards the question of immortality. He worked from a position of ignorance—a position that was unverified and that offered no security. His starting point was a subjective conviction about the good life, and it was held in the face of objective uncertainty.

The subject is an individual, but not just one entity among

a multitude of others. He is a particular, unique reality. Kierkegaard points out in *Fear and Trembling* that in the philosophical tradition, the universal has always been the absolute. It can be applied to all mankind. The highest goals are always the most universal ones. Kierkegaard, however, proposes a reversal of thinking on this issue and claims that it is the particular that should be considered absolute. Only in one's role as a single individual can he experience that which is most fundamental to his existence. Only as an individual in distinction from the universal can a man stand alone and in silence. In isolation, the individual comes to know who he is. He may not be able to make his actions comprehensible to others because he lives in increasing silence as he approaches selfhood. Kierkegaard comments that in the experience of subjectivity, one knows that

> there winds a solitary path, narrow and steep; he knows that it is terrible to be born outside the universal, to walk without meeting a single traveller. He knows very well where he is and how he is related to men. Humanly speaking, he is crazy and cannot make himself intelligible to anyone.[1]

The silence that Kierkegaard describes goes beyond language. The individual cannot bring what he discovers into the open. It is impossible for a man to speak of the experience of subjectivity, no matter how much he wishes to do so. He cannot attain the relief of speech, because his journey moves into the realm of paradox. The self is like a channel opening out to the sea, a channel that becomes increasingly difficult to see as it widens. When it becomes the sea, it can no longer be seen at all. The man who makes the journey to selfhood achieves subjectivity, but it becomes increasingly hard to single him out as he approaches his goal.

These suggestions about the self are expanded by the later Existentialists. Jaspers argues in *Reason and Existenz* that man is first of all an empirical existence, that is, an object of scientific concern. Then he becomes consciousness, in which he is an individual having common bonds with others. On this level, shared ways of thinking and perceiving predominate.

Finally, there is the level of spirit, which is neither the informational level of empirical existence nor the shared experience of consciousness. At this point, there are unifications and a sense of totality. Things are related in the context of the whole, and communication goes beyond a discussion of common likes and dislikes. But even on the level of the spirit, communication breaks down, and there is a movement towards an experience of transcendence. It is in transcendence that there is the fullest understanding of being, and it is here that the self comes into play. At this stage, man leaps to a form of transcendent thinking in which he recognizes his deepest self, including and going beyond all other forms of being.

One of the more extensive analyses of the self can be found in Sartre's chapter on the for-itself in *Being and Nothingness*. Having established the for-itself as one kind of being, Sartre proposes that the self is the origin of all negation. Nonbeing is the result of human freedom. Experiences such as questioning, imagining, and valuing pull man out of the chain of being and introduce possibilities into his world. For Sartre, as for the other Existentialists, the self is that which raises questions about being. By questioning, man defines himself as different from being-in-itself. He creates fissures or gaps between himself and his possibilities. His awareness of his freedom leads to anguish, which is the recognition that it is possible to do the opposite of what he plans or resolves. Because there is always a gap between motive and action, no human project has an absolute foundation. Man may try to flee the resulting anguish into deterministic explanations of his behavior; but the more he tries to escape, the more his anguish corners him. In the attempt to ignore anguish, he is confronted with his own bad faith.

Take, for example, the situation of a thief. He realizes that he steals but explains it by saying that he is a victim of circumstances. If he had not grown up in a ghetto, he would not have been tempted; his poverty and misery determined his fate. According to Sartre's analysis, this would be a classic example of the way in which the self moves from freedom through anguish to bad faith. The thief is the one who steals.

No one else is responsible for his actions. He is aware of this fact, but the anguish that this awareness creates causes him to flee into a deterministic explanation of his actions. The explanation is false and manifests the peculiar features of bad faith.

For Sartre, the self must be understood in conjunction with the notion of bad faith. In bad faith, man tries to escape anguish by denying it. He lies to himself, pretending that his anguish is not the consequence of his freedom. But this lie does not have all the features of an ordinary lie. It is a refusal to recognize certain aspects of one's being. The self is both the deceiver and the deceived, and yet it is one and the same self. But to be both the liar and the person lied to, a man would have to be aware that he is the victim of a lie, and this awareness is not ordinarily present in a situation of deception. A Freudian would explain bad faith by making the subconscious self responsible for the lie and the conscious self the victim. But for Sartre, this explanation begs the question. A lie is conscious behavior. If the subconscious represses the truth, it must be aware of what it represses; and if aware, it is conscious.

In bad faith the conscious self denies what it is. It either refuses to accept the facts of its situation, or it refuses to grant that it can alter its state. The first refusal is the self's denial of its *facticity,* a present situation, and the second is the denial of its *transcendence,* a possibly different future situation. The thief can ignore his facticity by claiming that he is not really a thief at all. His behavior is merely a temporary expedient until he gets a job. Or, on the other hand, he can ignore his transcendence, by arguing that his situation is hopeless. He decides that he will never be anything other than a thief; he is a confirmed criminal.

But at the same time that the self denies its facticity or transcendence, it lacks confidence in these denials. Thus the faith of bad faith wavers. At one moment the thief is firmly convinced that he is the criminal that everyone thinks he is; at the next, he loses faith in this stand. He jumps at evidence that is not persuasive—at the statements of others, perhaps, or statistics about thieves. His conception of himself is in flux because the self is split at its core; he cannot fully believe what he thinks he believes. There is an inner disintegration always at work, making it possible for him to be both the liar and the victim of the lie.

Sartre's description indicates a number of features about the self. The self is different from being-in-itself because of the structure of self-consciousness. All belief has a double element, since it is consciousness of belief at the same time that it is belief. In order to know something—a fact—one must be aware that he knows. Self-consciousness is this awareness. In self-consciousness the self is present to itself and therefore seems to have divisions within it. Yet these divisions only occur when one tries to understand the self. In fact, self-consciousness exists simultaneously with consciousness of an object. No fissure appears in the actual experience.

Sartre's discussion of the self can be supplemented by some points from Heidegger's analysis of *Dasein*. When man questions being, he finds that he already has some understanding of being. This is not only an awareness of possibilities but also an obscure sense of being in the world, a sense that the self can take hold of or neglect. This relation to the world is not fully grasped by scientific description. Science, in fact, must be based on an understanding of the self. But how does one arrive at a knowledge of the self? Knowing is not just one more physical property. It is internal—an attempt to grasp the unique way in which the self exists for itself.

Self-knowledge seems to be an impossibility. How can one person be both the knower and the known? Man has an intuitive self-awareness—an immediate sense of self. But is it accurate, and does it provide knowledge of the self in the same way that there is knowledge of a formula or knowledge of the colors of a rainbow? In fact, as Heidegger points out, man has a developed capacity for self-deception. If pursued, the immediate awareness of the self might be found to be made up of elements of pure fantasy.

But neither is it possible to turn to another person's opinions to implement self-knowledge. As Marcel suggests, the other may be biased. If, for example, one person tells another that he is good-tempered, is there any guarantee that the description is trustworthy? The latter may be counting on the former's friendship when he asks for information about himself. Any description coming from the other will be inadequate because it only indicates the reaction of another. It does not aid in self-knowledge. The question "Who am I?" has been converted to the entirely different question, "What is he?"

Marcel characterizes the self as "opaque." One cannot get away from himself in order to form an adequate picture. He presupposes his existence when he inquires into it. This is why it seems impossible to have self-knowledge. The questioner is caught in the attempt to know himself as a knower. As knower, he eludes his knowing self. Furthermore, he is always more than what his present self reveals. He is his possibilities in the future as well as his limits in the present. How can his knowledge grasp that which he has not yet become?

Sartre's answer to these questions is the proposal that there is no direct knowledge of the self at all. Rather there is reflection—an intermediate stage between intuitive self-consciousness and the knowledge of others and the world. In reflection there is an intrastructural modification of the self, made possible because of divisions in man's being. He is both what reflects and what is reflected upon. He looks for himself, trying to recover his being, but without becoming an object to himself. Reflection is a form of recognition in which the self is intuited as a quasi-object, partially but not completely detached.

Other Existentialists would take Sartre's point further and argue that the self is not even a quasi-object to itself. Marcel, for example, refuses to consider the self an object at all. When one says that he "knows" the self, what he means is that he participates in a presence. To move back to any kind of subject-object distinction is to undermine the earlier ontological insights. No individual is an object for himself, because his being cannot be split up into a subject and an object. Knowledge and being cannot be separated.

Some of the complexities of these theories of the self have to do with differences in emphasis. Sartre is concerned primarily with a description and characterization of the structures of the self; Kierkegaard, Jaspers, and Marcel are interested in the growth and development of the self. For them the self is an ideal as well as a fact. It is something towards which a person strives, and growth in knowledge is a part of this striving. Knowledge increases in intensity and value as the self becomes more complete. As the quest for being deepens, knowledge expands.

The question of the self gives rise to another issue—that of the body. Philosophers generally focus on the self as knower and give less consideration to the self's bodily existence. The Existentialists find this another of the damaging effects of mind-body dualism. If the mind and the body are considered separate substances, this makes it possible to stress one over the other. The issue of the body is directly associated with any question concerning the self. And since the body is bound to a temporal existence, to understand the body the philosopher must explore the meaning of time.

The Body and Temporality

The answer to the question, "Who am I?" refers to the body and to the existence of the body in time. It is a mistake to consider the body as though it were an object like other objects in the world. A unique relationship is sustained by it. One cannot separate himself from his body in the way he separates himself from a table or a chair. If he does view it as an object, he takes the point of view of another person towards it and looks at it *as if* it were the body of someone else. Yet even though the body is not an *object* of knowledge, every person has knowledge of his body. He sees his arm, feels pain, or hears his own voice. This issue is further complicated by the fact that the body is used to obtain knowledge of itself.

Marcel argues that the fact of being a body in the world is the most fundamental feature of an individual's situation.

Often in talk about the self, it is the body that is meant. The body cannot be an object, because man cannot dissociate himself from it in a way appropriate to objects. It is inaccurate to say, "I have a body." The body is not possessed in the same way that a car or a house is. Nor is it an instrument, subject to the same kinds of dealings as other instruments. Similarly, sensation cannot be conceived objectively as an elaborate transmitting apparatus. There is no translation or reception in sensation. This is because the self is a presence, having a subjective identity which cannot be broken into parts. Man feels himself to be his body and his sensations. He does not relate to his body; he participates in it as an incarnate being.

It could be argued that the body becomes an object if one commits suicide, but Marcel rejects this point of view also. Suicide is indeed possible, but it does not indicate that a person is something other than his body. In fact, it is only one more way of showing that he is his body. If he disposes of his body, he disposes of himself as well. There is no self independent of the body. The mind-body problem does not exist, because no split between the two can be found. It is possible to speak of different aspects of the self, such as feeling, sensation, or thought, but these are aspects only. They are not pieces of the self which have to be put together. Sensation belongs neither to the body nor to the mind. It is a form of human functioning, which has both physical and mental components.

Sartre discusses the body in relation to the existence of other people. The body has two modes of being. The first is its being for itself, and the second is its being for others. These are incommunicable levels and cannot be reduced to one another. When a person's body exists as an object for others, it is no longer the body of which he is conscious. Part of the difficulty in understanding the body can be traced to the use of objective models to describe it. Sartre claims that absolute objectivity is a myth that even science now recognizes. Experience cannot exclude the observer's relationship to the thing observed. Man and the world are relative to each other. One's body is part of his situation as an engaged being among other beings.

Sartre points out also that sensation is neither totally subjective nor objective. The warmth of water is a quality of an object, but it also gives information about the body that senses it. Pain is a way of apprehending both the world and one's body. The body can be understood as the center of reference for things in the external world. It is in relation to one's body that objects in a room are grouped. The window refers to human vision; the heat, to body temperature. If the window is opened, the room will cool off. It is because of the presence of the body that the window becomes an instrument.

Both Marcel and Sartre suggest in these analyses that the self *is* the body. Sensations are one way in which the body experiences the world, and the existence of bodily sensations is a condition of man's spatial organization of things. But the body also exists in time. Some of the Existentialists limit the analysis of temporality to a discussion of the past, as Marcel does, and all show particular interest in the past. Marcel approaches the question of the past in much the same way that he approaches that of the body. It is no more possible to objectify the past than it is to objectify the body. The past is not a succession of events; it is fluid duration. It cannot be understood by piecing it together. It is grasped through having participated in it.

Sartre's position is that the very structure of the self entails temporality. Man is the being who projects values and possibilities, setting up ideals that are not yet achieved. The past is an individual's past, related to his present and future. It only stops being his past when he dies, at which time, being congeals around him. The past is the growing mass of being that man secretes behind him. It is an accumulation of experience for which he is responsible but that he cannot change. The past acquires weight because it can no longer be retracted. Years that are gone are gone forever. They gather in back of a person, inalterable like being-in-itself. One can try to flee the past in bad faith, but here too bad faith fails. The past can be neither ignored nor changed.[2] The present is the self's presence to being. It is a flight from the past to the future, which is the state with which one will eventually unite. The past is dragged along towards the waiting future. And yet the future is only an ideal point, which, as it is being realized, slides into the past.

Sartre points out that there are two ways of looking at time. Impure reflection can be used, in which time is revealed as static. Impure reflection tries to make the self a thing, and time then appears as an irreversible succession of befores and afters. Pure reflection, however, distorts the self less, because it substitutes duration for multiplicity of discrete moments. It views temporality as dynamic so that past, present, and future are continuous. The self acquires a future and refuses a past—pulling the future into the present and evicting the present into the past.

Sartre's conception of time inherits a number of features from Heidegger's position. A large part of Heidegger's major work is devoted to temporality. Time is the standpoint from which the self must be interpreted. In fact, for Heidegger, being can be understood only if its temporal character is explored. Therefore, the basic issues of ontology are rooted in the phenomenon of temporality. The structures of the self must be interpreted as modes of temporality. Temporality even establishes man's spatial situation and is the foundation of his historical existence.

Inauthentic temporality for Heidegger results from the human tendency to become absorbed in multiplicity, thereby distracting man from the future. An inauthentic approach to the past would be the tendency to ignore what has been either because of a fear of the past or because of merely idle curiosity regarding the present and future. Time is construed as something public, happening to everyone, and therefore, of no particular concern to the individual. Inauthentic temporality is the attempt to escape one's self by a refusal to see what is the case.

But since the future is continuous with the past, inauthentic temporality falls short, in much the same way that Sartre's static temporality does. Heidegger indicates that the alternative, authentic temporality, allows man to understand himself. This may lead to anxiety because man often misses his goals. Only in moments of resoluteness can he hear the call of conscience. The future can make the past clear for the present self if the distractions of the present are overcome. The self then achieves an understanding of its own potentialities. Heidegger comments:

> Resoluteness constitutes the *loyalty* of existence to its own Self. As resoluteness which is ready for *anxiety,* this loyalty is at the same time a possible way of revering the sole authority which a free existing can have—of revering the repeatable possibilities of existence.[3]

Any consideration of temporality must include the question of death. The Existentialists consider death a philosophical issue of the first importance. Kierkegaard, in his use of the story of Abraham, introduces a number of questions that occupy the later thinkers. It is out of Abraham's confrontation with the possibility of his son's death that faith comes. Kierkegaard suggests a variety of ways in which Abraham could have reacted to the command to kill Isaac. But they are conventional reactions to death and therefore have no special meaning. Abraham is the man of faith because he expects the impossible—that he will retain his son. He abandons any kind of human understanding.

Marcel builds on the idea that it is through the confrontation of the death of another that crucial insights are gained. Death is a mystery, one of the experiences that cannot be grasped logically. If it is construed merely as a scientific fact, it is objectified and its meaning is obscured. Marcel's interpretation of death is that it is a trial, much as the command to Abraham is a trial. If one exists in a state of ontological lack, the presence of death is a sign to despair. This attitude changes radically, however, when self-realization takes place. The death of another is not a final absence. Rather it makes possible a reaffirmation of the presence of the other, through the experience of fidelity to the person who died.

But even more urgent, perhaps, is the question of one's own

death. It is here that Sartre and Heidegger offer the most complete analyses. Since death, for Sartre, is one feature of the human situation, it therefore has the same ambiguity that man's situation always shows. No person is responsible for the empirical phenomenon of his death, but since man is free, he is responsible for the character of his death. He gives meaning to the fact that he must die. He may ignore this fact or deal directly with it by the attitudes that he chooses to take.

Sartre also suggests that death is the triumph of the point of view of the other. When a person dies, he can no longer alter the other's conception of him. Others can call a person a coward while he is living, but there is always a possibility that he can change their opinion of him. He may yet do a courageous act or otherwise convince them that they are wrong. But once he is dead, they have the ultimate advantage. They can say anything they wish about him, and he can do nothing. Death, then, escapes one's projects and to some extent falls outside of the human situation. For while a person can have attitudes towards his death, he cannot realize them once he is dead. There is no way of arming oneself against death.

Heidegger's position has some of the elements found in each of the two conceptions already described. Like Marcel, Heidegger starts with the question of the death of another. It appears possible to grasp the totality of another's being if one observes that person's death. But the death of another is ambiguous. What does it mean to say that a person dies? The dead person can be more present in one's consciousness when he is dead than when he was alive. Death cannot be thought of simply as a termination.

But one's own death is equally ambiguous. It cannot be described as total destruction of the self because one lives on in the minds of others. Nor can it be considered the fulfillment of a life, since many die frustrated and unfulfilled. Heidegger proposes that death should be understood as a factual certainty towards which inauthentic or authentic attitudes can be taken. The inauthentic attitude defers thought about death to the future. In this way death is a public event, something that happens to other people, but about which one can afford to be indifferent. The authentic reaction, on the other hand, recognizes death as an impending possibility, which one can deal with only by anticipating it. It is one's own death; until one comes face to face with the fact that he must die, he is not free.

To understand the self, therefore, it is necessary to understand the body and man's existence in time. In talking about himself, a person puts himself in a temporal context. He refers to his childhood, commenting that as a child of a certain age, his behavior was of a particular kind. Or he speaks of himself in terms of his future projects. He is what he will be. One of the most influential attitudes that he has is his attitude towards his own mortality. He cannot separate himself from this attitude. Since death is the limitation of his projects and ideals, even his refusal to think about death is a freely chosen position. His body, his existence in time, and his death—all are part of what he is.

But there is another kind of being beside the temporal body and the self—the being of the world. Any theory of knowledge must propose a view of the relationship of the self to the world. How does one make contact with the world? Is knowledge of it like the knowledge one has of his body or his past? There also seem to be more and less satisfactory ways of describing one's relationship to the world. Some descriptions are true and some false. Questions about the external world and the problem of truth are closely related.

The World and Truth

There have been two major philosophical positions concerning the existence of the external world. One is that the world exists in complete independence of the self, and the other is that the world is reducible to the self. The Existentialists endorse neither of these positions, taking a stand between them. Heidegger and Sartre offer the most extended analyses of the world. They both point out that the world presents itself to man as something which he is not, yet it is he who gives it its character.

Heidegger suggests that the self's most fundamental feature is its existence in the world. The analysis of the world must be included in an analysis of the self, just as temporality must be included. Man only achieves self-understanding by exploring the world in which he finds himself. The notion of a completely external world is meaningless, since the world can only be understood in relation to the self. Man is in space and finds things in space—things that can be put to use or that resist use. The self gives things meaning by making them instrumental to its goals. It is man who contributes instrumentality to things in the world. He does not give a hammer its being, but he does give it its usefulness. It is because he is a being who can use a hammer that a hammer becomes his tool. Separated from man, entities in the world cannot be discriminated; they exist in an undifferentiated mass.

Heidegger pursues this theme in an analysis of the environment. An environment does not appear merely because it is perceived. It emerges as a result of human concern for things. Man finds entities that can be manipulated or put to use as equipment. The self understands the world without thinking about it. It isolates things and employs them as signs, tools, or equipment. It also arranges things in the world in spatial terms. They are established as being near or distant, or as having places. Knowledge is the means by which man makes contact with the world; it is his way of existing. He is able to assign places for things because he is a spatial creature. He knows that there are directions because he has directionality.

Sartre's discussion of the world follows Heidegger's in many respects but also develops Heidegger's position further. He begins by arguing that being-in-itself never *does* anything, it has no creative power. It is man who forms it into the experienced things of his world. He is responsible for any relationship that he establishes between himself and being-in-itself. Things are created initially by negation. A person finds that he is present to something that is not himself. When he says, "I am not that book," he is a necessary condition of the negation, but he is not its exclusive creator. He allows the thing to emerge as something in his world, but he does not add anything to the being of the thing.

The things of the world that are revealed by negation exhibit various structures. They have qualities, spatiality, instrumentality, and permanence. In particular, Sartre stresses spatiality. The book is spatially related to other things, appearing as a dominant figure against a background. When the book is isolated in the foreground, other things move back into the totality of being and are no longer discriminated. Things remain unrelated in the world until consciousness introduces spatial relations. The other structures of things are implied by spatiality. Quantity, permanence, quality, and instrumentality are all given at one stroke.

Not only are things of the world spatial; they have a temporal dimension as well. However, man introduces temporality to the world in a different way from that in which he establishes his own temporality. He assigns temporality to things, neither adding anything to them, nor taking anything from them. The past and future of a thing are perspectives given to being, which in itself remains atemporal. The time assigned to things, according to Sartre, is the time of the person who assigns it. If someone claims that his sailboat had a long past, the past that he gives to the boat is his own past. He points to the place where the boat was gouged by a rock, or he shows a spot of his friend's blood on the bow. The boat is revealed as having a past because its owner is a being in time. The boat reflects the owner's time. As being-in-itself, it is immutable and outside of time. Time is cast on its surface and flows over it without affecting it. Thus, things appear in the world and disappear—assigned an empty place in time by temporalizing selves. The self supplies the cohesion that enables a thing to have a past and a future.

The knowledge that man has of the world is, according to Sartre, immediate. It is a result of the self's presence to a world that reveals things different from the self. Knowledge is the intuitive presence of the self to these things. The relation of the knower to the known is what Sartre calls "pure denied identity." Just as an arc can be seen as either convex or concave, depending upon the observer's perspective, so the knower and the known can be imagined as two aspects of one and the same relationship. In claiming to know the color of a light, a person immediately intuits that he is not the light but that he is related to it. Knowledge is a negation, but there is a link between the self and that which it negates.

In their conceptions of knowledge, Heidegger and Sartre draw from both the Idealist and Realist traditions but do not affiliate with either. From the Idealists they take the emphasis on the self. Without human consciousness, there would be no things in the world. Being-in-itself would remain opaque and massive. But the self is not all that there is. From the Realists, they take the emphasis on the "worldhood" of the world, on the fact that something must be there for consciousness to negate. Sartre suggests that knowledge is intermediate between being and nonbeing. Its source is human, but if reduced to operations of the consciousness, it refers the philosopher to being.

As things in the world are articulated by the self, the question of truth takes on importance. There are ways of concealing the world as well as ways of revealing it. However, because knowledge is immediate and intuitive, the various forms of the correspondence theory of truth are unsatisfactory. For ideas to correspond to things in the real world, there would have to be an artificial separation between consciousness and things. To avoid this separation, Jaspers and Marcel work from the argument that truth is a value.

One of Jasper's introductory questions is, "What is truth?" He derives it from Kant's question, "What can I hope for?" There is a drive towards truth which is made more urgent by the breakdown in knowledge and communication. The philosopher hopes for more than dogma or scientific accuracy. Dogma is permanent and fixed in time; scientific accuracy satisfies only the intellect. A proposition can be logically satisfactory without meeting the deeper demands man makes in seeking the truth. These demands can be met ultimately only by the use of the symbol.

Truth is not something permanent; there are as many kinds

of truth as there are modes of existence. One works gradually through the more elementary forms to truth of a symbolic nature. Jaspers suggests that initially on the level of empirical existence, truth is pragmatic. It is relative and changing, serving the needs of the moment. On the next level, that of consciousness, truth is correctness, yielded by evidence. Finally, on the level of spirit, truth is the conviction that one has in a spiritual idea. The truth of each level incorporates that of the previous levels. However, even on the level of spirit, communication breaks down. Jaspers places the ultimate truth on an entirely different level, that of transcendence. Here is where the symbol is used, in the face of the inadequacies of language. "The ultimate in thinking as in communication is silence."[4]

Marcel develops a position that works from many of the same assumptions made by Jaspers. Marcel argues that truth is a value. His exploration is guided by some concrete questions. What does it mean to say that someone dies for the truth? Can a person's actions be guided by the love of the truth? Does truth purify? The correspondence theory is of no help, because truth of the kind referred to in these questions does not have to do with judgments. Nor is truth merely what is real. Things can be recognized as real but not true. When it is available to the truth, the self confers a "reverberatory" power on facts. A person opens his mind to a painful truth much as he opens his eyes to a blinding light. However, that which seems blinding may turn out to liberating. One can become a witness to that which was originally the cause of suffering.

Marcel suggests that Heidegger's conception of truth comes close to his own, particularly in its emphasis on openness. Heidegger, like Marcel, rejects the correspondence theory. Truth can in no way be demonstrated. It is the scandal of philosophy that it always expects proofs. In fact, proving of any kind presupposes a theory of truth. The correspondence theory argues in effect that truth is the agreement of a proposition with its object. But how can a proposition agree with a thing when they are so unlike? If one says that the statement represents the thing, the meaning of "represents" remains obscure.

Heidegger offers a view of representation in which a thing is represented when it is allowed to reveal its being. "'Truth' is not the mark of some correct proposition made by a human 'subject' in respect of an 'object'. . . . Truth is rather the revelation of what-is, a revelation through which something 'overt' comes into force."[5] The essence of truth for Heidegger is freedom. Truth is revealed when man makes himself available to what is. Freedom is the "letting be" of what is. The thing is uncovered by man's concern with it. Freedom is not the random exercise of caprice; it is a participation in the revealed nature of things. Untruth accompanies the truth because revelation presupposes concealment. The truth, or that which is revealed, presupposes that which is not revealed as well. Also, insofar as the self's being is inauthentic, dissimulation is fully as characteristic as revelation. Truth is always relative to man's being. Because there is truth only insofar as man is, the concealment of truth always accompanies the truth. Paradoxically, the revelation of what is turns out also to be the concealment of what is.

In discussions of the world and the truth, the Existentialists introduce a number of changes into the theory of knowledge. They point out how it is in the human encounter with the world that the various features of the world are revealed. But these features are not totally dependent on human will. Man discriminates things, but being is there first. He attributes to being those characteristics that suit his faculties of knowing and doing. What he cannot do is treat the world as though it were an easily classifiable object—one that can be completely described.

As a consequence, truth is not the exact correspondence of a thing to propositions about that thing. Propositions and ideas are only aids to be used in approaching the truth. Truth does not apply to them any more than it applies to the use of senses or feelings. All of these are means by which man opens himself to the truth. The truth cannot be willed. If man makes himself available to what is revealed, freely and without distraction, he comes closest to the truth. It is, then, a value, one that is related to communication. As Jaspers points out: "To be self and to be true are nothing else than to be in communication unconditionally."[6]

The introduction of the issue of communication leads to a final topic in the theory of knowledge, that of the existence of other people. When man communicates, he communicates with others. The majority of one's actions are designed with communication in mind. Knowledge includes the attempt to know others, and other people determine the character of many of the things which are known. In fact, man's being is always a being with others. Any understanding of the self not only must include an analysis of time, the body, and the world; it must also place the self in the context of its relations with other people.

The Other

No person exists in isolation; man is in community. Existentialist thinkers differ about the nature of the community, but all of them consider relations with the other to be a central feature of the self. The discussions of the other fall loosely into two groups: one in which the other's existence provides the ultimate realization of the self, and the second in which the other is a limit or barrier to self-realization. Although the issue of the other is an ethical as well as an epistemological one, the concern at this point is with its implications for the theory of knowledge. Questions of the body and the world also involve the other, since both phenomena are seen through the eyes of others. A person's body exists for others as well as for himself. His world can be enriched or impoverished by the fact that others influence it.

Jaspers' conception of the relationship between truth and communication leads directly to a discussion of the other. He characterizes philosophy as the growth of the individual in communication with others. The second question of Kant that Jaspers rephrases is the question, "What shall I do?" For Jaspers this becomes "How is communication possible?" It is not possible as mere togetherness. In togetherness there is a loss of significant universals. Here Jaspers parts company with Kierkegaard, who aims at suspending universals in the name of the particular. Jaspers argues instead that the problem is to find universals that are more satisfactory than those presently accepted.

The isolation of man from man is experienced in many ways—in the use of masks to hide feelings; in the failure to reach other people; in the inability to respond to appeals. Insufficiency in communication is a form of lack of being. To remedy this state, being with others must be reestablished. Only in communication with others is the self revealed. A person can be free only if others are free. But communication is not readily accessible, and it often breaks down. On the level of empirical existence, it fails because it is concerned with others as objects of investigation. On the level of consciousness, generalizations and universals are invoked, but they fail to deepen understanding.

On the level of spirit, Jaspers suggests a form of communication in which unity is the first consideration. The stages of acquiring information and discovering mutual likes and dislikes are transcended. One finds that the other fits into a total view of the self and the world. Jaspers argues, however, that even at this stage communication falls short. Perhaps this is because of the contingency of any human relationship. Or perhaps it is because another can never adjust perfectly to one's own vision of totality. Granted that it is through communication that man comes to be. Granted that the various forms of communication allow for increasing depth of relationship. Still, even at the most complete stage, an abyss is reached. That which goes beyond communication at this point is religious experience, and here there is a movement away from the personal self-other experience into an I-thou relationship with a transcendent being.

Marcel reaches a similar point in his discussions of intersubjectivity. He deals extensively with the false forms of communication. When people are massed together in a group, they are not intersubjective. They are alienated from each other—unable to make contact. Each individual is hardened into his shell and can only say, "I am," not "we are." The world is broken up, and a real community is impossible. There is only an external relation of entities. Each person takes what he can get from others, competing for a personal goal that he establishes in opposition to the goals that he imagines others hold.

Opposed to this state is the internal relationship of inter-subjectivity. Here the other comes within the reach of the self. The experience of being with the other may be the result of an ordeal experienced in common, or it may be a sense of a common future goal. When a person is related inter-subjectively to another, the other is present to him, making him more fully himself. If he is intersubjective, he is receptive and willing to give himself. There is a continual communication between oneself and the other.[7]

Marcel finds much in common between his position and that of Martin Buber in *I and Thou.* Buber also points out that the intersubjective or I-thou relationship can only be experienced by the whole person. The self claims nothing in this experience; the relationship is timeless. In particular, Marcel agrees with Buber's idea that the relationship is achieved finally through grace. Man makes himself available to the other, and waits to receive him. The I-thou relationship cannot be compelled.

Heidegger's conception of the other also begins from the view that man encounters the world in relation to others. The equipment of the world takes its character from those among whom one exists. Even when a person is alone, his being is still a being with others. The furniture that he uses, the food that he eats, and the tools with which he works have acquired their meaning as equipment for a group of people. It is because others have assigned a chair a function that it has meaning for him.

Man relates to the other with solicitude. It may be only a pretense at concern, or it may be a true attempt to free the other to himself. Knowledge of others comes as a result of being with others. Knowledge and empathy are possible only because the other has already been disclosed as someone with whom one exists. The relationship as described thus far by

Heidegger has similarities with that characterized by Jaspers and Marcel. But Heidegger goes on to point out that the experience of being with the other can be destructive as well.

The relationship with the other is a barrier to self-realization when it degenerates into what Heidegger calls the experience of the "they." This refers to man in general, an average that refuses to grant priorities or differences. If one wishes to avoid responsibility for action, the "they" is blamed. By assigning responsibility to the "they," the self can hide in a public image. This mode of being is one of inauthenticity and failure. However, Heidegger does suggest that there are ways of modifying the "they":

> If *Dasein* discovers the world in its own way and brings it close, if it discloses to itself its own authentic Being, then this discovery of the 'world' and this disclosure of *Dasein* are always accomplished as a clearing-away of concealments and obscurities, as a breaking up of the disguises with which *Dasein* bars its own way.[8]

Sartre, however, makes no such concessions. His characterization of relations with others refers exclusively to the modes in which the other limits and stifles the self. The other conditions one's existence, and any attempt to soften this fact is made in bad faith. Intersubjectivity and the I-thou relationship are sentimental ideals, not accurate descriptions. Analysis of the role of the other reveals that the other appears first as a mode of consciousness different from oneself. A being emerges that converts the self into an object. The first reaction to the existence of the other is shame, shame at appearing undisguised to the other's eye.

The other is first apprehended as a look, not as a body or an external object. The look by another fixes oneself as an object and can be countered only by the recognition that it is possible to look back. But before reconstituting oneself as a subject, a person cowers under the look. Someone, for example, may be watching a car accident with enjoyment, making no move to help. If another person appears and starts watching *him,* he experiences shame. The other pins him down in his embarrassment. He cannot explain or justify his behavior. He sees himself as he thinks the other sees him.

Also the other's look "steals" one's world away. Until the other appears, the car accident is constituted by the watcher. But now the scene is broken up and is part of another's world. It is no longer the same accident. It regroups around the look of the other. The world "hemorrhages" towards him. "It appears that the world has a kind of drain hole in the middle of its being and that it is perpetually flowing off through this hole."[9] The other's look, then, empties one's universe. The other seems to create all possibilities and to control all situations. There is no way to refer to the self except insofar as it is an object to the other. The other becomes the master, defining space and time, and alienating all possibilities.

Because he limits possibilities, the other is experienced as an obstacle. But he is not like an ordinary obstacle because he cannot be removed. His look is present everywhere, even though he may not be physically present himself. Even his absence is presence. A parent who is long dead can still exercise the power of the other over a child. The other seems to have infinite freedom as a subjective presence. Fear and pride as well as shame are reactions to this fact. One can try to re-exert his power as a subject, to convert the other to an object, and thus to subject him to the same treatment. Yet this attempt does not succeed; the other's freedom always reasserts itself. All he has to do is look back and the attempt to limit him collapses.

Sartre suggests a number of concrete attitudes that embody relations to others—attitudes that spring out of the fact of man's existence in the world. One of these attitudes is a result of the attempt to take the point of view of the other towards oneself. This attitude is manifested in a number of relationships, one of which is love. In the project of love, the individual makes himself an object for the other. But he is not satisfied merely to be an object; he wants to be a special object, one of unlimited value. As a result he tries to control the other's freedom. He proposes that the other freely constitute him as an absolute, uniquely desirable end. But this project is bound to fail. First of all, no human can ignore his subjectivity. He can never be a pure object. Second, insofar as he tries to make himself an object, he can only be one object among many, and he cannot have the unconditional value that he demands. Love then tends to degenerate into masochism, the attempt to ignore subjectivity altogether.

A second attitude towards the other is a reversal of the first. It is the attempt to make the other into an object. Love changes into desire, masochism into sadism. In desire, the other's subjectivity collapses. He is viewed as a physical object, to be appropriated at will. The other's freedom of action is ignored; he is used as an instrument. But this attitude also is unstable. The other can always reconstitute himself as a subject by exercising his freedom. Desire, then, becomes sadism, a last attempt to objectify the other through the use of violence.

But the other's freedom always remains out of reach, and every attitude that is taken is finally frustrated. The extreme of frustration is embodied in hate—resulting from the discovery that there is no way of uniting with the other or of salvaging one's own freedom. The project now becomes that of destroying the other—in fact, of getting rid of all others. But the other cannot be abolished because he persists as a look, surviving his physical destruction. For Sartre there is no escape from this circle of attitudes towards the other. One cannot neutralize the other's look. It is impossible to rest in intersubjectivity or to rely on communication. Man's condition is such that he lives in constant frustration, in which his freedom is always threatened but never disappears.

The problem of the existence of the other, then, is not the problem of other *minds*. The question of the knowledge of others is peripheral to the significant fact, that of *being with* others. Because man exists in the world with others, he acts in a certain way and has certain attitudes. The important concern is the nature of his behavior in the light of his situation.

Knowledge and Action

In summary, the criticisms and proposals offered by the Existentialists give new impetus to some areas of epistemology and eliminate others. There is an attempt to do away with the dualisms of traditional theories of knowledge—in particular, the mind-body and subject-object dualisms. As long as the subject is considered the knower, and the object the thing known, theory of knowledge remains at a standstill. Even language can be interpreted to support these dualisms.

Therefore, the very questions about knowledge are reformulated. The questions are changed so that the answers allow for the unities of experience. Theories of participation and reflection are substituted for the older conceptions of knowledge. Knowledge is a contemplative recovery of oneself and the world. The knower is not separate from what he knows. Instead, he is directly implicated in his subject matter—a participant, not an observer. The new conception of knowledge influences views of the self and self-knowledge. The self is not a subject that becomes an object to itself. It is a presence of which one is aware through immediate experience. There are occasional splits in the self, but these are internal not external. They are characteristic of the self's existence as a being that calls itself and its world into question. The self meets a world that seems to resist it, but at all times it is responsible for its choices.

The self is a physical being and a temporal being as well. Again, it is not a matter of viewing these aspects as objective. The body is not a thing, nor is time a succession of objective moments. Man *is* a body and he *is* in time. Both the body and temporality are experienced, not observed. One way of experiencing the body is through sensation, and one way of experiencing time is through the awareness of one's mortality. All of these modes of existence reflect man's being in the world and lead to an examination of the nature and meaning of the world.

The external world is not in fact completely external. It is man who is responsible for the existence of things in the world—for the fact that some things come into the foreground to aid his projects whereas others resist. The spatial location of things in the world is assigned to them by men. Since knowledge is man's presence to these things, truth is not simply an attribute of propositions. The truth about a thing is that which the thing reveals itself to be. For some of the Existentialists the content revealed is a value, which ultimately is communicated only through symbols.

Finally, the issue of communication leads to that of the relation of the self to others. Experiences of the self, the body, time, the world and truth are all conditioned by the fact of the existence of the other. Because the other is there, the world is different. The body is experienced in certain ways because of the other's existence. Knowledge of the self is developed in relation to the other's look. The other is considered sometimes as a limit and sometimes as an aid to self-realization. But in spite of this difference, both positions consider the existence of the other to be a significant datum for the understanding of the self.

For the Existentialists, therefore, every aspect of man involves every other aspect. His existence in the world is related to his being with others. Knowledge of the self includes knowledge of the body. Man is given in a situation as a whole. To take him out of his situation or to view him as composed of parts distorts his being. He is a self with others in the world, sustaining a bodily existence within a temporal setting. His knowledge is a reflective awareness of his situation—a contemplative participation in it for the purpose of gaining increased insight.

Another area in which the Existentialist theory of knowledge has unique features is in its close ties to value theory. The discussions of truth by Marcel, Jaspers, and Heidegger are directly related to ethical concerns. Also the various conceptions of the other have moral overtones. It is the other who aids or obstructs the realization of one's goals. One can deal with the other in good or bad faith, authentically or inauthentically. For the Existentialists, it is not easy to separate knowledge and action. Problems in epistemology concerning the self, the body, and the relation of the self to the world raise ethical questions as well. The knowing self is the acting self. Knowledge can be construed to be a form of action, and action is connected in turn to morality. The self exists as a valuing being.

5

Ethical Perspectives

Introduction

One noticeable feature of the Existentialist philosophies is the lack of systematic ethics. There is nothing on a par with Spinoza's *Ethics* or Kant's *Critique of Practical Reason.* Even when there is a well developed ontology, as in the writings of Sartre and Heidegger, one finds little attempt to formulate ethical systems. Kierkegaard comes closest to a treatise on ethics in *Either/Or,* but his discussion turns out to be part of a criticism of systematic ethical positions, consistent with his suspicion of systematic philosophy in general.

Traditionally, ethics has concerned itself with two major areas. These are what contemporary philosophers call normative ethics and meta-ethics. Normative ethics is the study of the nature of the good—usually a group of proposals about what the good life is and how it can be achieved. Meta-ethics offers judgments about the meaning of the proposals made in normative ethics. It analyzes the language and presuppositions of these proposals. For example, John Stuart Mill in *Utilitarianism* puts forth the normative precept: so act as to increase the general happiness. This precept is based on a meta-ethical principle that states that the good is that which is desired. Meta-ethical principles are often implicit in normative proposals.[1]

Normative ethics deals with three major questions. First is the question: what is the good? Second, why is it good? Finally, how does man persuade himself and others to be good? The first question asks for a proposal as to what man should do. The second seeks some reason or justification for this stand. And the final question concerns motivation. How is it possible to get people to be good? Once the description and explanation of the good are completed, there may still be a gap between understanding the good and doing the good. None of these questions is raised directly by the Existentialists, but neither is there an extensive critique of the traditional questions. There is, instead, a group of tentative offerings that are ethical in nature but do not present complete answers. The Existentialists consider the nature of value in detail and put forward some proposals about moral behavior. In many cases, however, these proposals are implicit.

The suspicion of systematic ethics can be construed as part of the general criticism of any fixed conception of man. Wilfred Desan comments, in a study of Sartre, that any formulation of the type "x is good" is a concession to the absolute. One becomes serious and proposes norms that cannot be transcended. Sartre's attack on the serious attitude bears out Desan's description. In the spirit of seriousness, values are considered eternal and independent of human subjectivity. Things are assigned the characteristic of being desirable. Man attributes values to objects and then assumes that this value was always part of the object. Because man has no established "nature," no one set of values can be assigned as definitive. His freedom makes it possible for him to choose values, but these values may be rejected once his situation changes.

For Sartre, the spirit of seriousness shows bad faith. It is a form of evasion, in which man tries to cover up the fact that he alone is responsible for the value he attributes to things. Serious ethics is an ethics ashamed of itself. It ignores man's freedom. It also assumes that man has a nature that never changes and that by a feat of magic, it is possible to make something good for all time and for all people. But in fact value is not absolute. Although man has values, there is no particular set of values that he of necessity should have. As Sartre comments, in describing his own development: "There is no salvation anywhere. The idea of salvation implies the idea of an absolute. For forty years I was mobilized by the absolute, a neurosis. The absolute has gone."[2]

Simone de Beauvoir in *The Ethics of Ambiguity* spells out this attitude. Serious ethical positions do not give man an adequate role. He is obscured in grandiose conceptions of good and evil. "The serious man stubbornly engulfs his transcendence in the object which bars the horizon and bolts the sky."[3] Idols are set up, robbing man of the meaning of his acts. With a conventional ethics man sits back and judges. In this spirit the present age condemns the Nazis, for example, without taking any responsibility for their actions. In particular Simone de Beauvoir agrees with Sartre in arguing that man flees his responsibilities if he posits an absolute universal. Since there is no such thing as "human nature," a value system cannot be deduced directly from a description of man. This position is a specific criticism of Kantian ethics. It suggests that Kant's categorical imperative makes it possible to avoid human responsibility.

Initially, the attack on Kant is somewhat surprising. Kant's categorical imperative, particularly in its later formulations, stresses responsibility and concern for human dignity. Man operates in a kingdom of ends—one in which the goals of the other are as fully respected as one's own goals. It is not this aspect, however, that brings about the critical reactions to Kant's position. It is rather the entire Kantian conception of morality. Kant argues that ethics is useless if it is relative. A relative ethics results in chaos in thinking and action. But on the other hand, one cannot legislate morality arbitrarily. Moral principles must be built from an understanding of human reason. The moral philosopher looks for universal laws that can be developed from a conception of human nature.

Kant maintains that man must be motivated to be good out of respect for the moral law. The source of that respect is reason. Reason disciplines him to abide by the law, and he gives the law authority. Man recognizes his duties and becomes a legislator. He therefore must create a law that has absolute power, a law without exceptions. Kant finds only one such law, the categorical imperative. "Act so that the maxim of your will could be universalized as a law." If an action is to be considered good, it must be possible to generalize the principle of the action, granting that any person could act from the same principle. Morality, then, does not merely advise; it commands. If it does not exact unhesitating obedience from everyone, it is worthless.

The rebellion against Kant's categorical imperative gathers force from the criticisms made by Nietzsche and Kierkegaard. Nietzsche's position on morality gives insight into the Existential attitude. His judgment of conventional morality is that moral systems are used largely to support emotional commitments. Moral philosophy is an elaborate form of self-justification, and rules are only tranquilizers. Worst of all, moral philosophies are boring. They offer an uninteresting Sunday-school morality and have nothing to do with the world. Morality enshrines weakness and timidity.

The herd-orientation that conventional morality introduces undermines creativity. Man lives in a moral temperate zone, carefully avoiding all extremes. Kantian morality offers man a sheep pen—comfortable, stuffy, and undisturbed. Nietzsche suggests that as long as man remains committed to herd morality, actions are leveled to one norm, and there is no freedom. Philosophy's task should be to upset, not to comfort. Religions of sympathy and compassion allow man to degenerate to the level of a gregarious animal. If man is ever to awake, he must step beyond conventional good and evil and commit himself to the unusual.

Kierkegaard also attacks Kantian morality but shows more sympathy than Nietzsche for conventional ethical positions. The ethical stage of human development is defended in the figure of a judge in *Either/Or*. The ethical stage is the classical stage as opposed to the romantic. There is a respect for law, achievements, and institutions. Choice is central to the ethical stage, and the personality concentrates on the universal. "One can choose oneself ethically only by repenting oneself, and only by repenting does one become concrete, and only as a concrete individual is one a free individual."[4] The man living in the ethical stage chooses himself as a definite individual, and he assumes responsibility for his choice.

The significance of the ethical life lies in the fulfillment of duty. The individual identifies himself with the universal and puts all of his energy to use in developing a vocation. He chooses actions in the name of the universal. Kierkegaard uses as an example the notion that it is the duty of every man to marry. Ethics cannot tell him whom he must marry, but it reveals to him the imperative *that* he should marry. The ethical man is, in effect, committed to Kant's categorical imperative.

But in spite of Kierkegaard's sympathetic presentation of this position, this is not the stand that he finally takes. In *Fear and Trembling,* he shows how the ethical stage of existence is unsatisfactory, and he argues for a "teleological suspension" of the ethical. The ethical establishes universal goals for all men. A person is judged in terms of the degree to which he governs his actions by law. But a fault in this attitude is that it ignores the individual. Because universal laws cannot explain the actions of the concrete individual, the ethical stage must be transcended.

The suspension of the ethical is not carried out on ethical grounds. A goal or *telos* is retained, but it is no longer ethical, and it is not a universal. It is purely private and personal. Thus, for Abraham, the highest value that can be generalized is the love of his son. But he goes beyond this into a realm where universalization of actions is no longer possible. His actions cannot be generalized, because of the purely individual and subjective nature of his experience. Universals are abandoned in the name of a higher goal—a goal that cannot even be communicated. There is no standard or measure, for there is nothing against which experience can be measured.

It is clear that Nietzsche and Kierkegaard reject Kantian morality. However, they do not negate all values. They criticize what they consider to be a degenerate form of morality, destructive to the individual. But there is another kind of morality that they endorse. For Nietzsche this is the transcendent morality of the superman. For the superman, there is a higher duty and responsibility. He stands apart and is capable of being different. The superman is the true aristocrat. Instead of repressing egoism, he celebrates it. The new morality does not generalize or claim that certain values are good for all. The superman's values are not for everyone. They entail suffering and self-assertion.

Kierkegaard's higher man is not Nietzsche's superman but has some similar features. For Kierkegaard, it is the knight of faith who transcends everyday morality. He goes beyond the conventional; in so doing, he can no longer be understood. He too exists in silence and suffering and abandons the commonplace. This man is not easy to identify because he does not look different. But he is different; he gives up all human commitments. He has values, but his values are those of the man of faith.

To some extent, the later Existentialists incorporate the criticisms of Kantian morality developed by Nietzsche and Kierkegaard. They look towards new values, having to do with the individual not the group. The disillusion with the older morality is expressed by Sartre, who comments:

> the moral attitude appears when technical and social conditions render positive forms of conduct impossible. Ethics is a collection of idealistic tricks intended to enable us to live the life imposed on us by the poverty of our resources and the insufficiency of our techniques.[5]

This attitude is one that has resulted from the attempt to derive an ethic from an ontological position on man's nature. Because, for Sartre, "human nature" is a myth, the attempt fails. Yet this disillusion with moral philosophy does not preclude the development of value theory. Sartre himself puts forward one of the more detailed theories of value.

Value and Anguish

The writings of the Existentialists discuss particular values as well as views of the origin and nature of value. Sartre's ontology gives rise to value considerations since he characterizes man as being engaged in a world of value. Ontology does not provide norms for behavior, but it does point out the sources of values and their nature. An analysis of man's being indicates a pervasive sense of lack. Consciousness is revealed as lacking things that are found in the world. In addition, it is aware that it is the origin of lack. Its structure is such that it desires to be that which it is not. Man's goal is to have the completeness of a god, but he always falls short of realizing this aim.

That which is lacked by consciousness is value. The existing self discovers itself to be inadequate. Value is the totality of being that man strives for but does not achieve. As a result, consciousness is haunted by value. For example, if one misses a piece of furniture in a room, the existing state of the room is unsatisfactory. Until the furniture is returned, the lack persists. The existence of that object in the room becomes a value—a totality that is desired. Man's total being can also be seen as a lack in reference to the self that he wishes to be. He desires to be a god-like complete entity, but his destiny is to remain incomplete. He drives towards perfection but can never achieve it; he suffers as a result. Even his suffering is not perfect. It is never quite deep and intense enough. He cannot become the perfect tragic figure. He sees himself playing at suffering and realizes that he is acting in bad faith.

Value is incorporated in man's being. It is a limit towards which he perpetually strives in the attempt to be different from what he in fact is. Even if one value is achieved, a new one emerges. As long as he is free, man can always imagine something that surpasses himself. The origin of value, for Sartre, could not possibly be a god or an external force. It is man who creates value, by his freedom. Since he knows that he can surpass himself, he posits ideals, which represent unachieved values. It is because a person does not belong completely to himself that value is possible. Value is absent possibility, projected into the future. A person always hopes to coincide with his goals, to be a great painter or a great musician. But once his goal is achieved, new possibilities emerge; the cycle persists as long as he does.

This aspect of the human situation allows no resolution. Because man is a temporal being, new horizons always stretch before him into the future. In the face of the frustration of goals and the inability to make values absolute, man experiences what Sartre calls "ethical anguish." This is the recognition that human freedom is always able to alter the values that it creates, and yet it can never change itself. Anguish results from the recognition of the fact that one is fully responsible for values and yet cannot realize them completely.

Sartre suggests that there is anguish only when there is freedom. Because of his freedom, man creates situations of nonbeing. He cuts into the causal chain of being by as simple an experience as a question. A question always presupposes a negative answer. When one asks what time an airplane will arrive, he implies that it is at least possible that no plane will come at all. Similar gaps, "holes" of nonbeing, appear between an image and an object or between a motive and an action. For all these gaps, man alone is responsible.

Anguish is the recognition of the full import of freedom. It is not fear of specific threats in the world. Rather it is apprehension following from the recognition of what freedom entails. A person can destroy his possibilities fully as much as he can create them. He can build a future in his mind, planning projects designed to implement his goals, but all the while, he can go on wasting year after year. It is possible to betray one's plans for the future, sabotaging the values that appear so easily within reach. Because one can always abandon a project, the future never seems to have a strong enough foundation.

One reaction to anguish is flight, aimed at escaping the consciousness of freedom. This could be flight into determinism, the claim that man is not responsible for his actions. Determinism is often an attempt to disarm oneself of responsibility. Flight can also take the form of a refusal to commit oneself seriously to future projects. Since it is possible that plans will not be realized anyway, why bother to try to fulfill them? But all such attempts at escape are in bad faith, since anguish is part of man's condition. The flight from anguish often has the effect of multiplying it.

The theme of anguish is not new with Sartre. As he points out, he is indebted to both Kierkegaard and Heidegger.* The concept is first developed by Kierkegaard and then pursued by others. For Kierkegaard, anguish is connected with man's reaction to a responsibility and freedom that he does not completely understand. Kierkegaard suggests that anguish originates in guilt and in the consciousness of sin. Man is aware of the possibility of infinite freedom and is overwhelmed by his potentiality to do evil.

But the experience of anguish is also a sign of man's growth towards being. The person who does not experience anguish is spiritless, stagnating in false contentment. When he experiences anguish, salvation becomes possible because it is through anguish that he recognizes the force and extent of his freedom. Only upon knowing anguish can the individual have faith. Until Abraham undergoes the anguish of recognizing the possible reactions he could have to the divine command, his faith is unreal.

Heidegger's conception of anguish develops Kierkegaard's distinction between anguish and fear, a distinction that is also used by Sartre. Fear is always fear of something definite. Anguish, on the other hand, has no specific object. It is indefinite and reveals nothing. It is, in fact, what makes fear possible. Man experiences anguish at being in the world. The world is always different from what he is. Out of this undifferentiated anguish, fear of specific things emerges. Heidegger also suggests that the experience of anguish is preliminary to authentic being. Most people distort anguish, losing themselves in the present and refusing to allow the world to reveal itself. They are engrossed in the superficial and turn away from nonbeing. But original anguish can be awakened at any time,

*In the standard English translations of the works of Kierkegaard and Heidegger, the words "dread" and "anxiety" are used instead of "anguish." For consistency, the discussion here uses the word "anguish" throughout.

by any unusual occurrence. "It is always on the brink, yet only seldom does it take the leap and drag us with it into the state of suspense."[6] The experience of anguish is a way of affirming the inwardness of things.

The discussions of value and anguish indicate considerable unanimity. Sartre points out that value is man-made, not found in the world. Even though the other Existentialists do not develop this point specifically, the theories of anguish suggest that to some extent they agree with him. Because of man's free encounter with the world, value is possible. Man is the originator of nonbeing, and consequently, he must take responsibility for the incompletion of his projects. As a result of his responsibility, man experiences anguish. He recognizes his ability to destroy what he creates and even his ability not to create anything at all. An immediate reaction to anguish is the flight into inauthentic existence, in which anguish is denied or converted into manageable theories. But genuine values can only coexist with the experience of anguish; if man lacks the courage to encounter his anguish directly, his values are degraded.

The introduction of the concept of degradation of values carries the discussion towards questions of normative ethics. Man's situation entails the creation of values, no matter what attitude he takes towards them. But values can be more or less satisfactory. They can be the popular values of the masses, or they can be the values of the realized self. With the classification of behavior into authentic and inauthentic, there is a question of what man should do, not merely of what he does. Because freedom and value are traits of man's situation, they themselves are neither good nor bad. But reactions to the situation vary. In inauthenticity, man tries to escape his freedom; in authenticity he accepts and uses it. What, then, is the justification of these values?

Normative Ethics

There are three major areas in the writings of the Existentialists from which to draw material for normative ethics.

One is the scattered group of suggestions made in the context of analyses of other subjects. A second area is the exploration of values in the context of literary works. The third area is the material on psychoanalysis and human development, found particularly in Sartre's work.

Three questions have been proposed as guides to normative ethics. What is the good? Why is it good? And how does man persuade himself and others to do the good? These questions are not meant to be binding and are introduced primarily to organize a large amount of diverse material. In spite of the criticisms of the ethical attitude and the suspicion of norms, there are many normative proposals in the writings of the Existentialists. This is largely because the critique of ethics is an attack on only one kind of ethical inquiry. For example, the refusals of Kierkegaard and Sartre to provide normative proposals is a rejection of the position that ethics is the categorical enterprise defined by Kant. This stand does not say that specific values cannot be advanced, but it does preclude an absolute or definitive moral position. Values can be suggested, but they are plural and particular, not universal and general. An ethical position must be set up in which values are not absolute.

Values cannot be deduced from ontology. As Sartre points out, ontology is only a springboard for ethics. It ends where questions of morality begin. Ontology provides a value theory upon which to build, but a theory of value cannot justify the choice of specific values. As the exploration of the good is pursued, it is found to have direct bearing on man's being. However, it cannot be derived from a description of being.

What is the good? At first it is easier to say what it is not. It is not inauthentic existence or bad faith. This behavior is dictated by the masses or by impersonal institutions. The inauthentic life is the result of losing oneself in the world and becoming preoccupied with one's own image. It embodies the refusal to take responsibility seriously. Responsibility for actions is assigned to others or to a generalized external object. The inauthentic state is one of lack of being, in which man falls short of his potential.

Inauthentic behavior is illustrated by the characters in Sartre's play *No Exit.* The three protagonists create their own hell by refusing to recognize themselves as they are. They try to save their false images of themselves by attempts to convince each other of the truth of these images. Garcin, for example, a deserter, offers descriptions that whitewash his behavior. In turn, the other two build an image of Garcin that is equally inauthentic and try to persuade him to accept their characterization of him. Inauthenticity operates both in the characters' views of themselves and in their views of each other.

Inauthentic behavior is superficial, passing its time in idle talk. It flees silence and loses itself in words, which, because of their misuse, give up their original meaning. The chatter of idle talk is an irresponsible attempt to avoid the past and future by incessant activity in the present. Marcel's play *The Broken World* presents a heroine who experiences such irresponsibility. She finds that her world has run down, much like a clock that needs repair. She goes through a ritual of meaningless performances in the social world that she has chosen. The image that she has tried to fit becomes increasingly empty.[7]

Another manifestation of inauthentic behavior is illustrated by the irresponsibility of the romantic, who takes life as a game. In Kierkegaard's "Diary of a Seducer" he illustrates the inauthentic behavior of the aesthetically oriented personality. The life of the seducer is revealed in his letters, in the course of which he describes the seduction and subsequent abandonment of a woman. His life is motivated by the enjoyment of the beautiful moment, with no attention to the future. The seducer resembles a beast stalking his prey, which, once obtained, is set aside.

Kierkegaard's description of the seducer suggests that inauthentic behavior is directly connected to interpersonal relationships. Inauthenticity makes it impossible to recognize what the other is or can be. The other is converted into an object to be used and discarded. There is no realization that the other has claims or freedom. By generalizing his object, the seducer no longer considers her an individual at all. Her acquiescence is merely a sign of his victory. As soon as she gives in, the beautiful moment has passed, and he seeks a new prey.

The inauthentic person refuses to see himself and his world clearly. Inauthenticity is manifested in the misuses of language, in bad faith, in the inability to recognize the role of the other, and in the rush of everyday activities. In a state of inauthenticity, one appropriates others; he does not try to understand them. Curiosity and distraction predominate. Inauthentic behavior is a form of uprootedness. The inauthentic person is not at home; he has fallen out of being. Falling leads to temptation, tranquilizing, alienation, and self-entangling—a downward plunge into the groundlessness of inauthentic everydayness.[8]

Heidegger and Sartre both argue that their descriptions of inauthenticity and bad faith are not ethical in nature. Yet despite these disclaimers, both philosophers suggest that there are degrees of such behavior, and that to some extent, one can transcend these states. If this is so, the discussions of inauthenticity and bad faith move into the area of normative ethics. In authentic behavior, a person recognizes who he is and makes an attempt to move towards his being. The "they" is no longer used as support or justification of action. Idle chatter drops into silence, a silence that says more than the original noise. The authentic person comes to grips with his freedom and takes responsibility for his projects. He is not controlled; he controls. Possession is less important than being.

The status of the authentic personality is illustrated in Sartre's play *The Flies*. Both Orestes and his sister Electra illustrate forms of inauthentic behavior, but one sees in Orestes a conversion to authenticity, as he begins to take responsibility for his actions. Although Electra is not able to recognize the implications of the act that she urges on Orestes, he, on the contrary, realizes the full import of what he does. He does not have to run from the harpies, who represent the anguish of recognition of responsibility. His courage lies in the full acceptance of their presence and therefore in his willingness to take responsibility for his action.

If authentic behavior is a good, why is this so? The second

question of normative ethics is more difficult to answer than the first. It asks for reasons in an area in which no completely coherent explanation can be given. The justification for considering authenticity a value cannot be transcendent because this takes responsibility for values away from man. Nor can one justify norms by an appeal to a conception of human nature; man does not have a nature.

Justification of norms is never entirely satisfactory because man's situation is absurd. Camus suggests that the world of values is neither predictable nor controllable. It is an irrational world, and there is no ultimate meaning to human existence. A gap persists between man's intellectual constructs and the universe. Conditions hem him in, isolating him from the world in a way that cats and stones are not isolated. Man lives without appeal. He cannot justify new values by appeal to convention. Nor can he appeal to his role. He cannot say that he does things because he is a member of a class that has always done those things. He must make a leap into action without support. He is a stranger, trying to create meaning, but always faced with the abysses of the irrational. He rebels against authority and against others but can give no ultimate justification for rebellion.

However, the concept of absurdity does not eliminate the possibility of justification of values. It only implies that no absolute justification is possible. On a different level, justification may be introduced. The concern is always with the existing individual. In questions of values, it is to the values of the concrete individual that the philosopher turns. He avoids the established theories and examines himself for the source and defense of his values. The authentic is recognized as the good because of an individual's immediate awareness of it as such. But immediate awareness is a shaky criterion by which to justify values. How can the inauthentic self trust its evaluations? The answer to this question of justification is linked to the third question of normative ethics: How is one good? For a number of the Existentialists, the experience of conversion is instrumental to the achieving of values. A conversion from the state of lack to a state of authenticity takes place. There is an appeal or call from conscience, stimulating this conversion.

That which is called by conscience is the self that exists in the present—the inauthentic self. Because the self is able to reflect on itself, it is possible to be receptive to an appeal to be different. The obscure sense that one has, that he can be other than he is, allows a state of receptivity to exist. Man exists in time and can always be something different from what he presently is. His ability to project a future state makes it possible even for the inauthentic self to be reached by an appeal of conscience. More difficult is the question of what calls. Is it the authentic self, present in embryo? There is some disagreement on this issue. Marcel and Jaspers suggest that it is the real or authentic self that makes the appeal. The real self is hidden by inauthentic modes of being. When freed, the real self emerges; when submerged, it is experienced in the appeals of conscience.

The positions of Heidegger and Sartre are more difficult to determine. The self is what makes the appeal, but it is not a hidden real self. Because there is a fissure in the self's being, it is possible for there to be an internal dialogue in which the recognition that there is a future is incorporated into a judgment of the present. For example, a child may endorse his parent's goals for a long time without questioning them. He will be a scientist as they always said he would. But he begins to recognize that his goals are not authentic. He has neither the ability nor the interest to be a scientist. That which makes this recognition possible is the awareness of alternative possibilities. He could be a mechanic, or for that matter, he could be a bum. It is not necessarily his real self that appeals to him; it is the awareness of future possibilities that initiates the change.

A condition of hearing the appeal of conscience is receptivity or availability. Most of the time hearing is dulled. People seldom change radically. But conversions do take place. Authentic hearing is at least possible. The obstacles in its way are numerous. One can become trapped in egoism or in institutional demands. Inauthentic behavior appears much more prevalent than self-realization. One tool by which hearing the call is facilitated is suggested by Sartre. His theory of existential psychoanalysis is designed to aid in clearing away some of the obstacles to conversion. Sartre bases his conception on his conviction that man defines himself by the ends he pursues. An analysis of these ends makes possible an understanding of the fundamental project behind them, the irreducible project that is at the core of all human behavior.

The underlying principle of existential psychoanalysis is that man is a totality and has an immediate sense of himself. The goal of analysis is to conceptualize behavior patterns by comparing individual actions. As these actions are explored, they indicate the way in which the individual realizes his fundamental project. As long as he blinds himself to the nature and meaning of his behavior, conversion is impossible. But if, through existential psychoanalysis, he can uncover the manner in which he lives out his goals, conversion can take place. He can isolate forms of inauthentic behavior and substitute new ways of realizing his fundamental project.[9]

Sartre describes conversion as a radical change in one's entire being:

> These extraordinary and marvelous instants when the prior project collapses into the past in the light of a new project which rises on its ruins and which as yet exists only in outline, in which humiliation, anguish, joy, hope are delicately blended, in which we let go in order to grasp and grasp in order to let go—these have often appeared to furnish the clearest and most moving image of our freedom.[10]

One can prepare for conversion by the analysis and understanding of secondary projects, but existential psychoanalysis cannot cause conversion to take place. Marcel and Jaspers suggest that at this point one can only be receptive to grace. But this stand is based on religious presuppositions that Sartre does not accept.

The normative values that emerge in this discussion remain tentative and incomplete. They are values that are tied closely to the conception of self-realization. The authentic self is the realized self—the self that *is*. In conversion, the self is recognized, as the disguises and limits of inauthentic existence are abandoned. The description of the way in which such values are achieved leads back to the question of why authenticity is a good. It was suggested that a person has an immediate recognition that certain kinds of existence are good and that this recognition is all that is necessary for a justification of individual values. The theory of conversion indicates one way in which this immediate recognition can be judged reliable.

In conversion, the self is fully present to itself. In inauthentic states, there is considerable distraction. In both cases there is a sense of the self. But authentic existence reveals fewer discrepancies. The cycle of bad faith is not present. The projected goals of the self are immediately recognized as authentic and are not met with conflicting goals that undermine them. In authentic behavior one immediately recognizes those things that are good. Difficulties emerge when goals begin to conflict, and it is at this point that existential psychoanalysis becomes necessary.

The questions of what the good is, why it is good, and how to achieve the good become merged in Existentialist ethics. The authentic is good because it is recognized as such in the course of conversion. Inauthentic behavior is judged to be unsatisfactory in the light of the self's goals, which can be clarified by means of existential psychoanalysis. There is no exterior or transcendent justification of the values that are proposed. The justification that is most acceptable comes from the direct experience of these values.

In his characterization of conversion, Sartre points out that this experience offers one of the most dramatic representations of human freedom. The issues of freedom and responsibility are directly related to normative ethics. It is because man is free that he creates values. His freedom is what makes conversion possible. When man fully recognizes his freedom, he is responsible as well; when he refuses to take responsibility, he falls back into inauthenticity.

Freedom and Responsibility

Although there is a unanimous rejection of traditional theories of freedom, the Existentialists do not all agree about the nature of freedom. The conceptions that will be discussed in detail are those of Marcel and Sartre. The positions of these two philosophers represent two distinct points of view, but even if full account is taken of their disagreements, their stands have a considerable amount in common. Both of them attribute to determinism some of the characteristics that have been traditionally assigned to fatalism. In their criticisms of determinism they do not give their conceptions religious traits, but they do suggest that the deterministic position precludes the possibility of man being a determining agent in his own life. This resembles a fatalistic argument, suggesting that man's efforts have no effect whatever on his future.[11]

Freedom is not a matter of simple choice between two alternatives. Marcel points out that this conception leads to the opposition between freedom and determinism. If the free act is the selection of one alternative over another equally possible alternative, freedom is put on the same level as determinism. Freedom becomes just one more factor in the determination of an event. It is a mode of causality and turns out to be a disguised determinism. The attack on determinism is carried out at length by Sartre. Whereas Marcel criticizes determinism for its objective view of human experience, Sartre rejects it because of its misunderstanding of the nature of causation and motivation. Determinism makes no distinction between motives and physical causes. It ignores the fact that the nature and weight of motives depend on the meaning that a person gives them. Determinism tries to make the self a thing by suggesting that consciousness is externally motivated. As a result, the self is confused with the world.

Sartre points out, however, that there are contributions by brute existence to a person's situation. One is born into a particular race, at a set time, in a definite place. He can do nothing to change these facts. But he does give these facts their meaning by the goals he establishes. That which is given is always illuminated by his freedom. Although a person receives his place as a specific location in space, it is through his freedom that he gives meaning to that place. He chooses his place in the light of his ends and is therefore responsible for the place he takes. Or again, one's environment is the grouping of the instrumental things that surround him. The adversity of things is illuminated by his freedom, even though the environment remains indifferent. It is the unpredictable, resisting world, but its resistance is foreseen. Freedom gives meaning to the contingency of things in spite of the fact that it adds nothing to them. It merely causes them to manifest themselves as out of reach.

Another position that is criticized is the view that freedom is the use of the will to control desire. Marcel describes this position as one in which the agent supposedly deliberates about possible courses of action, calculating the advantages of each alternative. The reasons for acting in one way rather than another are decided upon, and then a particular action is willed. This position assumes that man's freedom is manifested in the power of will. Will is pictured as a faculty that fights desire.

Marcel objects to this position because of its assumption that experience can be calculated and controlled. No person knows exactly what the ramifications of a choice will be, nor can he fully decide what is in his power. Often only after the fact does one recognize that an act has been free. If one decides to visit a sick friend, there is no way of knowing how he will feel or act during the visit. His attitude may change significantly upon the actual encounter, and the whole previous calculus can be upset. To say that a simple decree of the will determines consequent actions is to oversimplify experience. In many situations a calculation of possibilities cannot be made. Marcel does not maintain that deliberation about possibilities is irrelevant to action. Rather he maintains that that is not what makes the action free.

Not only is the assumption about the character of experience faulty. In addition, the accompanying view of the nature of the will is unsatisfactory. The will is made into a force or quantitative power. In using the will, man tenses in the same way he does when he uses his muscles. This suggests again the mind-body dualism in which the experience of the body is the model for a conception of the will. Also this position sets up the will in opposition to desire, leading to unfortunate ethical consequences. If a person is free only when he opposes his desires, he is not free when he yields to them. He then forfeits responsibility for many of his actions. He detaches his desires from himself and transfers the responsibility for his actions to an external force.

Sartre, too, objects to the conception of will as a power that opposes desires. He suggests that freedom is often considered a property of the will, whereas the passions are viewed as determined. There is, then, no way for the determined passions to act on the spontaneous will. In addition, this position implies that passions are not autonomous. In opposition to this stand, Sartre argues that the will is not a privileged manifestation of freedom. Both volitions and passions are subjective attitudes by which man attains his ends. Will refers to the reflective aspects of a project, and passion refers to the emotional aspects. Both of these are attitudes developed in the larger context of freedom. A person may have the project of writing a novel. Some of his attitudes are reflective. He reasons that his novel will make money or that publication will secure him a job. These attitudes are volitional. But he also may be driven by the fantasy that his book will be the great American novel. This attitude is passional. But both volition and passion are only ways of naming attitudes that are already present. They do not cause behavior.

The notion of voluntary deliberation is deceptive. A person has already conferred value on causes and motives before he deliberates. By the time he deliberates, the chips are down. Deliberation is only a way of making his project known to himself. The will is just one psychic structure among others. They are all supported by an original ontological freedom. Sartre argues that causes and motives are given their value by the self. The agent organizes a situation into complexes of causes and motives. The cause is the reflective reason for the act, objectively viewed, and the motive is the subjective desire pushing one to accomplish the act. They often exist together and can only be revealed through a person's project. Causes, motives, and ends are all part of a unified whole, expressing the free consciousness.

The criticisms of various views of freedom suggest the direction that the positive positions of these philosophers take. Marcel considers freedom to be a value, which must be won. For freedom to be achieved, it is necessary to resist the world of functionalization and dehumanization. The affirmation that is essential to the free act is the one that forms the person. Freedom is creative affirmation of the self. But a person can also refuse to be free. He can be confronted with the possibility of freedom and refuse to actualize it. Freedom then exercises itself in the act of betraying itself.

Marcel also argues that freedom cannot be considered apart from the concept of grace. Grace is a gift that can be neither demanded nor summoned. Yet without it, freedom is reduced to a caricature. With grace man is assisted towards transcendence of the constraints of his existence. It is on this issue that Marcel most strongly objects to Sartre's conception of freedom. He claims that by excluding the ideas of grace and receptivity, Sartre gives freedom a totally negative connotation.

Sartre's position does differ from Marcel's in a number of ways. He argues that no person is free to cease being free. Freedom is the very stuff of man's being. It is manifested in all human projects. Any person's acts are consonant with a broader meaning that is his life style. This is his project—the way of life that he chooses. The smaller choices are secondary. In fact, his very situation is made possible by his freedom. He discovers the resistance of others and freely encounters it in the situation. The situation exists only in correlation with the surpassing of that which is given. Man makes himself.

Freedom is inseparable from responsibility. Without freedom responsibility would be meaningless, but man cannot choose not to be responsible. He may try to avoid his responsibility or ignore it, but he is no less responsible because he chooses to live in bad faith. Sartre argues that responsibility covers all human actions. Each person is responsible for himself and his world. He is the author of the war that is being waged, of crimes that are being committed. He deserves the world in which he lives because he gives it meaning. He cannot claim that he is an innocent victim or that the world is not of his making. His choices make his world, and he is condemned to be totally responsible for those choices. Man is the being who is compelled to decide the meaning of being.

> The one who realizes in anguish his condition as *being* thrown into a responsibility which extends to his very abandonment has no longer either remorse or regret or excuse; he is no longer anything but a freedom which perfectly reveals itself and whose being resides in this very revelation.[12]

The question of responsibility leads to the consideration of social philosophy. If one's responsibility extends to the entire peopled world, he is confronted with social and political institutions that he must choose to accept or alter. The question comes up as to whether there are any grounds for finding some institutions more satisfactory than others. The ethical suggestions of the Existentialists carry over into the realm of social philosophy, but the conclusions that the different philosophers draw from these suggestions are not at all similar.

6

Towards a Social Philosophy

Introduction

If a person is a free agent, he is responsible for his actions. Since actions are conditioned by the existence of others, responsibility cannot be restricted to one's own behavior. There is responsibility towards others. Because an individual's actions affect other people, he always acts in a community. He is a social being and acts in good faith only when he takes responsibility for the effects of his behavior on others.

Some of the Existentialists also maintain that every person is responsible for the actions of others. This is a step beyond the argument that one is responsible for the effects of his own actions. Sartre argues this position, pointing out that an individual is accountable for the actions of people whom he may not even know. The action of the other is inseparable from one's own action. Every person contributes towards making the other what he is. An American cannot argue that a foreign war has nothing to do with him. His freedom chooses that war, fully as much as it chooses the activities of the next day.

There is concern for both social and political action. The conception of social action will be stressed here, however, as being the more inclusive category. Whereas some of the Existentialists are committed to specific political programs, others deal with questions of broad social import. They are critical of the way in which social issues have been treated by previous philosophers, and they extend their criticisms into discussions of the present condition of social institutions.

Conventional social and political philosophies raise problems of interest but deal with the problems from a limited and overly abstract point of view. The traditional conceptions of right, obligation, justice, the state, punishment, and the contract leave out a major factor, that of personal engagement. The problem of justice is real only if the philosopher in question engages directly in the issue of justice. If he is concerned with punishment, it must be from the point of view of someone who understands guilt. This viewpoint may be the reason why interest in social philosophy appears late in the philosophical careers of some of the Existentialists. Marcel and Sartre deal with social and political thought after the publication of their major philosophical works. For Sartre the change in focus can be linked to his experiences during the Second World War and the post-war period. Marcel's commitment to a political stand evolved gradually out of his activities during the First World War. There is, in both cases, a significant connection between personal development and the emergence of a social philosophy.

But even if the philosopher of necessity exists with others, does this mean that he should actively seek engagement? Why does the fact of his being with others obligate him to consider social problems? Sartre suggests that part of a sense of community comes from the fact that people unite with others into an "us-object." For example, to visitors, convicts in a penitentiary become an us-object—an object that experiences' common shame or resentment. As a group they no longer exist solely for each other but are an object for the spectator who comes to observe them. Each one solidifies with his fellows, and they stand as a unified community watching their observers.

But if an individual stays on this level, he does not become engaged in action. He is like a thing, existing to be manipulated, studied, or observed. This is the situation of oppressed workers, who exist as an us-object in relation to a landlord or a dictator. It is in terms of common misery that they are collectively apprehended by others as an object. The move towards engagement or social change must come out of the attempt of the oppressed to convert their state from that of being an us-object to that of being a "we-subject." They see the oppressor as an object, thereby introducing the possibility of destroying him.

Engagement occurs when there is a conversion of oppressed individuals into a subjective community. They become members of a group, with common goals and a common desire to revolt. However, this explanation of the origin of social commitment has difficulties, which Sartre himself acknowledges. The state of the we-subject is unstable. It does not really explain action. A person could imagine that he is a member of a subjective community of pacifists. He finds common goals with others and experiences an intense mutual emotion. But this could be nothing more than his own feeling, which he projects onto others in a wave of enthusiasm. The sense of unity is at best only a symbol of real unity—a subjective impression only. The experience of the collective subject, then, is not the basis of action. Sartre suggests that this experience is only a provisional appeasement, not the solution, of a conflict. It reveals the particular historical situation of a group, but it does not show why and how commitment to social change takes place. Often the community of the oppressed seems more stable than the subjective community of we-subjects.

To understand the nature of commitment to social concerns, the philosopher has to ask the more fundamental question: What is action? To be engaged, one must be able to see the possibility of modifying the world. He experiences an objective situation that he hopes to better. In order for change to take place, he must be able to act. So the issue of social responsibility is turned back to that of the nature of human action.

Theories of Action

Kierkegaard does not present an extensive theory of action, largely because the question of action falls into the realm of the ethical. It is the tragic hero who thinks and talks about action. Although the knight of faith acts also, he cannot discuss his action or construct a theory about it. His action is carried out in the context of the absurd. It is impossible to explain it or to make its nature clear. There are signs, however, when the action is that of the tragic hero. Oedipus is blinded; Hamlet shows weakness. The man in the ethical stage reveals laws, and his actions are based on the fact that they are actions that everyone would take. Because the realm of action focuses on the universal and on institutions, it entails the communication of values and attention to results. The good citizen acts; he expects his work to pay off. It is guided by a human form of reasoning, in which accounts are carefully balanced. One works towards the achievement of goals. But for Kierkegaard, this is only an intermediate stage. The individual must go beyond the realm of action to discover that the universal is not enough. A sense of the absurd leads to the experience of anguish that turns man towards faith.

More positive theories of action come from the later writers and lead directly into questions of how an individual alters social situations. Marcel suggests that philosophers often avoid commitment to specific positions because political topics seem impure or not truly philosophical. Or if this extreme is avoided, there is the other extreme in which philosophers become involved in a program without seeing all of its implications. Before any position is taken, the philosopher should understand the nature of action. Marcel goes on to point out that the act is what changes a situation. It is more than a mere occurrence or performance. The essence of the act is to commit the agent. Without responsibility, there is no action. This is because there is a solidarity between a person and his acts. It is the person who acts, not the depersonalized "one." The personal context of the action indicates that no man can repudiate his action without denying himself. Furthermore, there are times when he *must* act. Not to do so would make him "the guilty participant in an inexcusable blunder."[1]

Heidegger's conception of action has some features in common with that of Marcel. Heidegger claims that it is easy to maintain oneself in the everyday world. People perform actions constantly. The world is one of commerce and practical activities. But if man remains fixed in the everyday, he lacks the insight to understand his basic possibilities. On the level of the "they," man is content to satisfy rules and to be guided by public norms. He does not listen to the call of conscience because he is lost in present opportunities. Authentic action is not just what happens to the self; it is what the self brings about as a result of recognizing its own potentiality for being. In action, man "goes towards" himself.

Sartre's view of action is closely related to his conception of freedom. Traditional theories of action suggest that man acts when he interrupts the deterministically governed emotions by introducing controls from the will. Sartre, on the other hand, argues that both the will and the passions are means to goals that have already been established. Action modifies the condition of the world and manifests human freedom. For the self to have projects, it must be an agent. Through his acts, a person is known, since by these acts he arranges means in terms of his ends.

Action is always intentional. The careless smoker who causes an explosion does not act, but the dynamiter who causes an explosion does act. One need not necessarily foresee all of the consequences of his act so long as a conscious project is realized. Action is a result of a judgment of the present situation as lacking. The dynamiter imagines that the workers in a factory will be aided by sabotage. The present is inadequate, and his behavior is an intentional effort to remedy a lack.

No factual state can motivate an act. Insofar as one is immersed in an historical situation, he cannot imagine how his state could possibly be different. If his misfortunes appear natural, he will never act. It is his subjectivity, not the objective situation, that creates the lack. He conceives of a different state of affairs, and his suffering becomes unbearable.

Workers who are ruthlessly oppressed can imagine nothing other than their condition. Their suffering alone cannot be the motive for an act. They must withdraw in relation to the suffering, positing an ideal state and then comparing their actual situation to that state. An act is a projection of the self towards what it is not. The worker must wrench himself away from his world. Then his suffering becomes a motive for revolutionary action.

There is no act without a cause, but Sartre maintains that the cause does not come before the act. It is experienced as part of the act. The self observes the act and gives causes and motives their value. The value is assigned in terms of the goal of the action. It is by moving away from a situation towards its possibilities that the agent organizes the situation into complexes of causes and motives. The dynamiter, in characterizing his action, might claim that a cause of the action was the availability of explosives, and a motive was his desire to remedy social injustice. But in fact, the cause, motive and action are all one totality. Each gives the other its meaning. The act decides its ends and motives.

Action, then, includes more than mere activity. Both Marcel and Sartre agree that the agent distances himself from a situation and judges it. In the course of judgment, he projects a goal. This goal is inseparable from the motives and causes that are isolated in subsequent descriptions. A person takes action when he is able to reflect about his state and to accept responsibility for it. His act is not determined, but it is caused. The agent decides the causes of the act through his freedom.

Sartre's conception of action also appears in his ideas about the nature and function of literature. In the interview about *The Words*, Sartre comments on the relationship between literature and action. He indicates that part of his reason for writing *The Words* was to show how he had made an absolute out of literature and how it was possible to move away from literature towards action. He says, in relation to his early works, "I have changed since. I have had a slow apprenticeship to the real. I have seen children die of hunger. In the

face of a child who is dying, *Nausea* has no weight."[2] Literature must be universal and put itself on the side of the great-
est number. It must pose the problems sharply—cathartically.
The writer has to write for the many who are hungry, not
just for himself.

In an earlier essay on literature, Sartre makes a similar
point. In speaking, the writer acts. This is secondary action,
but action nonetheless. The writer chooses to reveal the world
to others through the use of words. If literature engages in a
cause, it is not weakened but enhanced. Once the writer
reveals a situation, it becomes more difficult for his readers
to pretend to be ignorant. In writing, the author appeals to
the freedom of the reader. His words may not act directly
on the reader, but they can be a condition of the action that
the latter takes. In appealing to the reader, it is inevitable
that the writer will embody the values of his class. But if he
identifies uncritically with the ideology of the ruling class, his
literature is sterile. Ideally, the writer's adventure should be
the same as that of the reader. But until there is a classless
society, this is impossible. Because of congealed hierarchies,
there remains a distinction between the writer's subject matter
and his public.

Writing, as a form of action, entails responsibilities. One
such responsibility is to clarify the reader's consciousness of
his own situation. The writer can goad a society to self-
criticism by provoking a guilty conscience. He appeals to the
reader's freedom, hoping to evoke understanding and col-
laboration. In turn, the reader becomes responsible for the
final work. But the writer is not licensed to endorse tyranny.

> It would be inconceivable that this unleashing of generosity
> provoked by the writer could be used to authorize an in-
> justice, and that the reader could enjoy his freedom while
> reading a work which approves or accepts or simply abstains
> from condemning the subjection of man by man.[3]

In these comments, however, Sartre no longer limits himself to a description of action. He proposes a particular kind
of action. This carries the discussion back to the question

raised earlier: How does the philosopher justify the type of social change he endorses? The fact of commitment is explained by man's condition as a being who acts. But a discussion of the nature of action does not show why certain actions are chosen over others. For an explanation of the social commitments of the Existentialists, one must turn to their analyses of social conditions.

The Present Age

One kind of justification for the Existentialists' demand for social change is implicit in their judgments of contemporary society. Kierkegaard, Marcel, and Jaspers, while speaking from different points of view, come to many of the same conclusions.[4] One pervasive theme in their discussions of society is that of the loss of inwardness. Instead of turning within to understand himself, man scatters his attention about him, trying to fill his existence with activities. In running from idea to idea, he fails to encounter the most important ideas—those of self-realization, communication, and transcendence.

In part, this situation results from a deification of science. Science in itself is not evil, but the uses to which it is put can be destructive. While it should reflect the application of reason to reality, it in fact becomes the slave of human desires and fears. Instead of being controlled, science controls. One sign of this reversal is technical progress, which proliferates without accompanying progress in the development of the individual. Any technical progress should be balanced by an effort at inner conquest and self-mastery. But instead, progress merely provides man with instruments of destruction. Technological developments tie man to the present, causing a breakdown of continuity with the past. The present age no longer has a sense of its history. Often hostile to his past, man remembers without assimilating. So the meaning of history changes also. It reverts to the abstract naming of events, a neutralized version of the past. There is a gradual loss of contact with the sources that nourish life.

The soul of the past event is obscured by the spirit of

abstraction. It is easy to generalize and reflect about an event, much easier than to crystallize the generalizations into concrete action. Although abstraction is necessary to clear the ground for planned action, it can also indicate contempt for the concrete. When a leader speaks of the death of thousands, his abstraction allows him to forget the individual. The particular death of one person becomes irrelevant. The form and method of abstract knowledge are available to everyone, but the ability to forge knowledge into concrete responsibilities is a neglected skill.

From abstraction it is only a short step to the functionalization and dehumanization of man. To some extent, man lets this happen to himself. To perform great acts is too difficult. It demands elasticity to struggle against the techniques of degradation. Confronted with the struggle, the individual abdicates, preferring to enjoy the comforts of technology and the benefits of a despiritualized world. Daily affairs are carried on according to fixed rules, and the person is submerged in his function. He is the sum total of what he produces—only as indispensable as the product for which he is responsible.

This situation hardens, and what first seems to be only a desire to remain undisturbed becomes a way of life. The prevailing materialistic world view is a sign that the individual is losing touch with himself. He is the victim of forces that no longer are under his control. Self-respect becomes an anachronism, since the self is a machine with a finite output. If one falls short of expectation, he can be scrapped and replaced. The material world that may have presented itself at one time as a desirable end is now the instrument of self-destruction.

Depersonalization does not make man any less talkative. If anything, he is more so. But his chatter shows a fear of silence, or perhaps the inability to be silent. With the passing of any significant distinction between talking and keeping silent, propoganda increases in effectiveness. It is a method of seduction easily subject to the uses of fanaticism. When words are designed to intimidate, man becomes a slave to them. The fanatic takes advantage of this servitude, basing his propaganda on contempt of those towards whom it is directed.

"A revolutionary age is an age of action; ours is the age of advertisement and publicity."[5] With these words, Kierkegaard introduces the conception of the mass man. As man seeks consolation in company, the notion of a public, the "they" or the "mass" becomes real. But this public is an abstraction. One can address an entire nation in the name of the masses and yet these masses will be less than a single person. The mass has an unstable unity, a mass apparatus, in which the rules made by a few dictate to the many. As a result, culture is leveled to the average.

One sign of this leveling is the use to which the communication media are put. Since journalism is dependent on the needs of the masses, the press becomes the tool of public opinion. For the fanaticized consciousness, the press is an ideal organ. It can refuse to recognize the competence of individual opinion, even though it contributes to forming opinion. The individual is confronted by a cycle that traps him. He cannot express a variant viewpoint because the media present him with no alternatives. His opinion appears to be formed without any contribution of his own.

The predominance of the mass idea can be traced to a misuse of the theory of equality. Equality is an ideal, supposedly on a par with liberty and brotherhood. But in fact, it is a concept that destroys the other two. It is used to justify leveling, in which each person is urged to be like others. Standards are held in common in the hope that unity will result. But to use the concept of equality in this way is to ignore the fact that unity is based on human dignity, not on the equalization of values. Equality turns out to mean little more than conformity. The process of equalization can influence areas long supposed immune. In the loss of any distinction between the private and the public, artistic production becomes gossip, and art is reduced to engineering skill. The revolt against aristocracy is more than a revolt against social injustice; it is also a rebellion against legitimate distinctions between the productive and the sterile. Mass opinion takes only a short view of its world and its culture.

The quality of work is affected as well. There is a loss of joy in work if activity is equalized. Jaspers finds an illustration of this situation in the relationship between doctor and patient. Insofar as medical treatment is depersonalized, the doctor remains unfulfilled, because he is no longer guided by a human image. The patient is a machine to be repaired and therefore he must be treated mechanically. The patient furthers this condition by demanding that he be repaired whether he is functioning poorly or not. The doctor is caught in a dilemma of which he is partly the cause and partly the victim.

The loss of individuality is found in an even more striking way in the functions of the state. If equality becomes paramount, true leaders are unrecognizable. The great are obscured by the clever or the powerful. It can be argued that a major role of the state is to enable man to build his own life and to fulfill his occupational ideals. But this can only happen if the state expresses the will of its citizens. If the leaders are unable to reflect the ideals of the individual, a tension develops between the leaders and the people. Each side paralyzes the other, and the state stands against its constituents.[6]

Kierkegaard summarizes the present age in the following way. It is an age of formlessness, in which principles are external. It is an age of superficiality, which has disposed of any distinction between that which is concealed and that which is manifested. It is an age of flirtation, which has eliminated the distinction between debauchery and love. And it is an age of reason, which has abandoned the distinction between subjectivity and objectivity.[7]

What is the role of the philosopher in the present age? He cannot speak as a prophet. This attitude would be an undue pretension to power. But he can promote understanding of the contemporary situation. His interpretation of life can indicate the extent of the possible, partly by revealing the actual. If man comes to understand his own uprootedness, he is in a position to transcend this state. Insofar as the sciences tend to veil man rather than to reveal him, the philosopher is in a position to point this out. He can provide a comprehensive view of man's science, his art, and his history.

But the idea of the philosopher has also been degraded. Often the philosopher is unable to define the limits of his own knowledge. He is tied to performance—the publication of technical articles or his appearance at academic conferences. One of his foremost tasks has been to mediate the world to man, and only if he can recover the meaning of this role will he stand outside of present techniques of degradation. Although he cannot prophesy, the philosopher can point. By denouncing the spirit of abstraction, he is in a position to show the dangers of insulation.

The many features of the present age point to one pervasive characteristic: the inability to take significant action. It is difficult for man to know what his real task is. He has science at his command but does not know how to use it. He has complex tools and equipment, but these tools menace his very existence. He has material comforts but is homeless—uprooted from his history. Man is detached from being, unable to realize himself. In the name of what hopes are these criticisms of the present age made? What is the home from which contemporary man has exiled himself? The criticisms that the Existentialists develop are rooted in a conception of a different future. This conception allows for the recovery of the sense of the past, the re-introduction of significant universals, and the humanization of man. The criticisms, then, imply positive programs.

The Solutions

The solutions to the difficulties raised vary considerably. Although the Existentialists have much in common in their evaluations of the present situation, their proposals take radically different directions. On the one hand, there is a conservative movement, represented by Marcel and inherited, to some extent, from Kierkegaard. On the other hand, there is the neo-Marxism of Sartre that proposes solutions with no resemblance to those offered by the first two. In the middle are the positions of Jaspers and Heidegger.

Marcel suggests a return to aristocracy but not to aristocracy in the traditional sense. The seeds of this conception can be found in the writings of Kierkegaard and Nietzsche, both of whom condemn the leveling devices of democratic and socialistic ideologies. They call for a renewal of creativity and individuality. Kierkegaard proposes a return to an age of intensive enthusiasm in which the individual who stands alone is the true aristocrat. The aristocracy that Marcel admires is a situation in which utilitarian techniques are mastered but then transcended. Technology takes its place as a means only, not as an end in itself. The true nobility is the group of independent individuals. It is a nobility of spirit, making up a new aristocracy, created by the work of the individual. The state reassumes its role of supporting the choices of the individual.

Concretely spelled out, the new aristocracy may indicate the return to monarchies or the renewal of small social units such as the family. It may be embodied in a return to the earth, in which man regains his roots and re-experiences his past. There must be a re-creation of living tissue, which grows in the small community in which honor is still important. Aristocracy is built on pride in independence and on hospitality. Marcel urges simplification and craftsmanship as aristocratic ideals.

The conservative nature of these proposals is suggested by the interest in renewing values held at earlier periods. Marcel's writings often embody a sense of nostalgia for a mode of existence that no longer prevails. They appeal for a recovery and preservation of concepts of self and society that were built with attention to man's humanity, not out of ignorance or destructiveness. Some of Heidegger's suggestions indicate a similar conservatism. He proposes a relationship between philosophy and history that aims at preventing man from losing himself in the mass. The spiritual destiny of the Western world has become a falling out of being—a loss of the sense of historical destiny. To renew this sense, man's spirit must be reawakened by an exploration of the nation's destiny in time.

For Heidegger, this reawakening takes the form of developing a new philosophy of history. History is not concerned with that which merely passes. It has to do with acting and with being acted upon. History is determined from the future and is a taking over of the past. Specifically, this means that the highest destiny of man lies in the realization of a national identity. If his nation lacks being, its citizens lack being also. Man must recover his being by establishing himself in a national community with close ties to the land.

Jaspers also argues that a conception of history is at the root of any recovery of man from the destructiveness of the present age. History indicates a movement towards unity, yet man's concern for his fellows has been retarded by the misuses of power in totalitarian states. Jaspers proposes that freedom will only be realized in a community in which men converse and plan together and in which their protection is guaranteed by constitutional and democratic devices. Unless the individual participates in the life of the whole, the whole becomes repressive. One man can be free only if all are free.

Concretely, for Jaspers, this end can be exemplified in a democratic community working towards world unity. Freedom requires unrestricted dialogue—something that is precluded by any ideology that pretends to be universal. Ideally, socialism would guarantee this freedom, but its present forms claim a total knowledge that can in no way be justified. Present socialistic communities have not protected political liberties, largely because of planned economies and unwarranted illusions as to the extent of human abilities. Jaspers proposes that through the use of democratic principles, world order is possible. This unity, however, can be achieved only by negotiation, not by the exercise of arbitrary political power.[8]

For Sartre, all the positions discussed thus far are inadequate. Sartre repeatedly points out that in choosing for himself, a person chooses for all men. His action is a commitment for all. One cannot make liberty his aim unless he makes the liberty of others his aim as well. A conception of aristocracy or of a return to a national destiny would be an abdication of responsibility. These positions show bad faith because they take no account of oppressive social and economic forces. If there is to be a criticism of the present age, it should be a criticism of the mentality that allows class discriminations to persist, sustaining inequalities.

In Sartre's major work on social and political philosophy, *The Critique of Dialectical Reason,* a central task that he sets himself is that of reconciling his theory of freedom with one form of Marxism.[9] Sartre rejects contemporary interpretations of Marx in an earlier essay, "Materialism and Revolution."[10] He judges materialistic metaphysics mistaken in its attempt to eliminate all subjectivity. Materialism may be acceptable as a human attitude, but it cannot stand as a rigorous philosophy. Much of Communist doctrine has become trapped in the inadequacy of its metaphysics and is unable to find a way out of its difficulties without causing dissension within the party.

One reason for the attractiveness of materialism, Sartre claims, is that it provides a deterministic catharsis. But it turns out to be an ideology more suited to the oppressor than the oppressed in that it allows the oppressor to view the worker as a machine. It cannot survive as a revolutionary philosophy because it does not permit a plurality of freedoms. Human reality is action, and the revolutionary is one who goes beyond the material conditions of his situation, projecting himself into the future. He needs a philosophy that can show how a situation can be changed, and this philosophy must be based on a conception of free human action.

In the *Critique* Sartre shows how Existentialism can provide Marxism with the necessary theory of freedom and action. Existentialism, similar to all other philosophical positions, is a way of putting knowledge together. No philosophy is absolute. Each one arises out of certain needs and movements in society. It can exist as a vital expression only as long as the particular social situation demands it. Because of its origin at a point of crisis in Western thought, Existentialism has particular features that the Marxist can put to use. A major difficulty with Marxism, Sartre claims, is that it moves too hastily towards totalization. Contemporary interpreters of Marx are guilty of over-abstraction, a tendency that is not found in Marx. If Marxism is reduced to *a priori* dictates, facts are forced to adjust to principles that never change. General dialectical descriptions of class movements can never show why two members of the same class develop in different ways.

One feature that Existentialism can contribute to Marxist ideology is its grasp of the individual in his concreteness. Through existential psychoanalysis, one can explore how a particular individual relates to his class. Childhood is not ignored, as it tends to be in Marxist thought; it is the starting point for existential psychoanalysis. Sartre proposes a "progressive-regressive" analysis in the study of the individual. Every person lives in an objective historical situation. This fact cannot be ignored. But also each person surpasses that situation towards the future, transcending the given and thereby making history.

In order to understand the concrete individual, the philosopher must inquire into that person's class but also consider the way in which the person places himself within that class. Any one action reveals two sides. If a member of a middle class family refuses to prepare himself for a white-collar job, this act can be seen from two points of view. From the viewpoint of the objective situation, this person's class contributes to making him what he is. His very rebellion is the rebellion of a bourgeois. But from another point of view, he is an individual refusing to accept the limits of his class. The collective apparatus of society is not sufficient to explain him. It is necessary to examine the actual choices that constitute the way in which he lives.

Existentialism, then, offers to Marxism a cross-reference in the description of the individual. Whereas Marxism emphasizes conditioning or economic forces, Existentialism refers to biographical studies and personal statements. Particular acts reveal a person's conditioning; one cannot talk about conditioning in abstraction from these acts. If the aim of a social science is to rediscover man as he really is, no structures should be neglected. That which is objectively given, the social whole, the personal individual project—all show how a man makes history by pursuing his personal ends.

Sartre argues that if there is to be an anthropology, it must be an Existentialist one. But it is Existentialism combined with a dialectical interpretation of history. Man's situation in relation to the modes of production can be approached in terms of existence. A rigid mechanistic determinism is unnecessary to situate man in his class and in history. If Marxism can eliminate its dogmatic metaphysics of nature and reintegrate man into its ideology, Existentialism will no longer have any reason for existing. It will have contributed its primary notion—that human reality freely makes itself.

While this discussion only indicates the skeleton of Sartre's social philosophy, it does suggest how Sartre proposes to integrate Marxism and Existentialism. He goes on in the *Critique* to show how, working with the principle of scarcity, the philosopher can come to an understanding of a variety of concrete situations. Some of the other Existentialists consider the direction that Sartre's thought takes to be a betrayal of Existentialist principles. But Sartre might argue that they are taking him to be more orthodox a Marxist than he is. He repeatedly dissociates his view from Communism or from any totalitarian ideology. It should be stressed that Sartre makes a distinction between the writings of Marx and later interpretations of the Marxist position. He understands the original writings in terms of a view of man that allows for humanitarian goals. This is a stand that is radically divorced from many contemporary Marxist commitments.

In spite of the diversity of the proposals made by the Existentialists, they have one feature in common. This is their concern for the freedom of the individual. Whatever direction social philosophy takes, a persistent theme is that the political and social situation must be such that liberty is assured. The individual must not be kept from existing freely in all of his uniqueness. It is also the case that their positions on social issues are closely related to their views on religion. Sartre, in "Existentialism Is a Humanism," argues that it is because God does not exist that questions of freedom and responsibility arise. Since there is no God to create a fixed human nature, man must make his own nature. His values are his own doing. Social institutions are a result of human responsibility.

Jaspers and Marcel connect their social philosophies explicitly to religious positions. They point out that the society that they endorse is modeled on the relationship between the creator and the created. All authority is ultimately grounded in transcendence. Political and social ideals are based on freedom, and freedom is related to grace. It is from a religious stand, therefore, that many of the social proposals originate.

7

Interpretations of Religion

Introduction

Critics often distinguish sharply between religious and atheistic Existentialists. This distinction is deceptive, largely because it suggests a precise division into two camps. Although some of the Existentialists themselves speak in these terms, the division is misleading. It is less a matter of a split into two conflicting parties than one of differences of attitude towards religion. These differences are not precise in all cases, and they point to a variety of approaches rather than to established positions. Those philosophers who are often called atheistic—Sartre, and occasionally Heidegger—are close to the others in some of their attitudes towards religion. Their criticisms of bad faith and inauthenticity in religious experience are criticisms that Kierkegaard, Jaspers, and Marcel would also endorse. Heidegger's position on grace and openness resembles that held by Marcel, and Sartre's conception of conversion has some interesting analogues in Kierkegaard's writings.

It is true that Kierkegaard, Jaspers, and Marcel make statements of religious belief that Heidegger and Sartre are not willing to make. But both Heidegger and Sartre understand human goals in a way that is similar to religious conceptions.

The fundamental project, as Sartre defines it, is man's desire to be God. Sartre's description of the inevitable frustration of that project resembles Kierkegaard's conception of anguish. Heidegger's writing remains ambiguous on the question of religious belief, but he does point out that his position is not a declared atheistic one any more than it is a theistic one. The dimension of the holy, he argues, is a closed dimension until the question of being is clarified. For this reason, he assigns himself the task of exploring the truth of being, rather than dealing directly with religious experience.

The philosophers whose positions are considered religious are not entirely happy with this classification either. Even Marcel, who is most formally committed to an orthodox religious position, rebels against the view that his philosophy is that of a Catholic. He argues that he developed his major ideas prior to his conversion to Catholicism. He points out:

> It is quite possible that the existence of the fundamental Christian data may be necessary *in fact* to enable the mind to conceive some of the notions which I have attempted to analyse; but these notions cannot be said to depend on the data of Christianity, and *they do not presuppose it.*[1]

Marcel claims that he cannot philosophize as though Christianity does not exist, but the Christian ideas must be thought of as fertilizing principles only, not as dogma.

Kierkegaard and Jaspers find many of the institutional aspects of religion too restrictive for their purposes. Kierkegaard rebels against theology and argues for a religious experience that transcends the limits of the church. Both Kierkegaard and Jaspers refuse to accept absolute approaches to religion. They consider dogmatic historical religion unsuited to the present age—particularly insofar as it claims privileged access to the truth. Religious experience is ongoing and exploratory, as are other forms of experience. Therefore the tenets of any religious position must be tested against experience, fully as much as principles in any of the other philosophical fields.

Interpreters of Heidegger and Sartre consider these philosophers atheistic partly on the basis of two essays: Heidegger's *Introduction to Metaphysics* and Sartre's "Existentialism Is a Humanism." In Heidegger's essay, considerations of a religious nature occupy only one section. He introduces this discussion by pointing out that if a person views the Bible as divine revelation, he already has an answer to the fundamental question before it is even asked. This person accepts unquestioningly the idea that all things are created by God.

Heidegger maintains, in this discussion, that the believer who decides to adhere to an orthodox religious doctrine has, in effect, made the decision to stop questioning. He acts as if it were possible to question; but in fact, if he really raised questions, he would cease to be a believer. He cannot, therefore, be both a believer and a philosopher. The philosopher must deal directly with phenomena he finds in his world, whereas the believer finds ways of passing over these phenomena in the name of conventional religious explanations of the world. The fundamental issues, then, cannot be raised by the believer. He defines man as a rational animal but makes no attempt to base this either on interpretation of observed phenomena or on an examination of the nature of being. From the standpoint of religious faith, Heidegger's fundamental question of metaphysics is meaningless. It is a question that, for the believer, is already answered.

In this essay, Heidegger is not saying that faith is meaningless. He is suggesting that the attempt to buttress faith with theology and dogma destroys any adequate foundation for faith. Faith is obscured in theological interpretations of man and the world. Theology, because it cannot sincerely raise the basic ontological questions, lacks a solid base. For Heidegger, a faith, to retain its strength, must perpetually expose itself to the possibility of unfaith. If it does not do so, religious belief is no more than a convenience. Theology, then, becomes a barrier to the dimension of the holy, not a pathway.

Sartre's essay, "Existentialism Is a Humanism," develops this line of thought further. Sartre points out that his position does not accept any religious claims; but this stand is not taken casually, or merely as a game. If the philosopher argues that God does not exist, he loses a major support of human values. When the existence of God is denied, it is no longer possible to base values on the imperatives of a divine intelligence. Because there is no perfect mind to think about or create the good, man is forced back upon himself to justify his values. There are no *a priori* principles to justify them.

Sartre's position attempts to take seriously the implications of denying the existence of God. He does not spend time disproving the existence of God. His brand of Existentialism considers both the proofs and disproofs to be idle exercises. "It declares, rather, that even if God existed that would make no difference from its point of view."[2] The real issue is not that of God's existence but of man's realization of his goals and recognition of his responsibilities. If God is excluded, man is left to establish his own values. He is no longer able to hide behind a transcendent being.

Sartre's position in *Being and Nothingness* bears out these points. He declares that man's fundamental project is to be God. But it is a project that always falls short. The religious ideal has deep origins, but it is not an actuality. Because of his recognition of the powerful influence of this ideal, Sartre often uses religious imagery to describe human experience. Most of this imagery, however, is used to illuminate forms of frustration. Sartre implies that the religious experience is an attempt to relieve frustrations that are built into the human condition. But because these frustrations are a part of man's condition, religious claims cannot be verified. They seek to provide a moral holiday when no such relief from responsibility is possible. The imperatives that man introduces are all of his own doing.

Neither Heidegger nor Sartre develop an elaborate criticism of religious beliefs. They point out the ways in which theology and religious experience are forms of bad faith, but they do not criticize specific religious doctrines in any detail. For this reason it is difficult to consider them militant atheists. They find contemporary types of religious belief outmoded as explanations or justifications of human behavior. They can be considered nonbelievers, but only because they do not believe in conventional religious dogma.

Heidegger and Sartre are not opposed to all forms of religious experience. They use a number of concepts that the "religious" Existentialists use as well. The category of transcendence, for example, is used fully as much by Heidegger and Sartre as it is by Jaspers and Marcel. The conception of human freedom is one that is emphasized by all of the philosophers in question. And the notion of anguish, while originally given a religious setting by Kierkegaard, is picked up by Heidegger and Sartre and used extensively. Instead of considering Sartre and Heidegger "atheistic" writers, it is more useful to say that their writings do not emphasize religious experience. In no sense do they go out of their way to be atheists in their major works; and insofar as they explore man's most basic projects, they are analyzing what the other Existentialists deal with under conventional religious categories.

Another reason why the split between the two groups is unsatisfactory is that both are equally concerned with eliminating forms of bad faith in human experience. This includes religious experience as much as any other kind. Jaspers, for example, finds the conception of the divinity of Jesus unacceptable for reasons similar to those one might find in Sartre. Jaspers maintains that it is a notion that inhibits inquiry and puts up a barrier to the experience of transcendence. In another direction, Marcel rejects the idea that religious beliefs are discontinuous with philosophical beliefs. He argues this position on the grounds that to isolate religious experience is to suggest that a privileged elect is closer to the truth than the unenlightened majority. This is a form of arrogance inconsistent with the philosophical enterprise.

Kierkegaard, Jaspers, and Marcel all depart from conventional approaches to the philosophy of religion. To understand the force of their rejections of traditional viewpoints, it is helpful to examine how some of the problems have been formulated in the past. Traditionally, one of the fundamental issues has been that of the existence of God. The proofs for the existence of God—in particular, the ontological proof—have held the attention of almost every major Western philosopher since the Middle Ages. The philosophy of religion focuses on this problem; and for some of the Existentialists, the question of the proofs of God's existence serves as the starting point for their own discussions.

However, other concerns also cluster around this issue. Whereas the question of the existence of God is a question about the object of religious faith, it also implies that there is such a thing as faith. This raises the issue of what faith is and whether it is different from more everyday forms of belief. There are many objects of belief, some of which are more trustworthy than others. Does religious faith introduce an element that is not present in the belief that the sun will rise or that fire will burn?

Ordinary beliefs are tested by reason and experience. Belief in the properties of fire can be verified. When a belief claim is made, the sceptic asks for either empirical or rational justification. But the person who holds religious beliefs is in a difficult position. He cannot give immediate perceptual evidence for his beliefs, and his rational attempts at proofs are often met with equally cogent disproofs. The questions of knowledge and justification, then, are important to any philosophy of religion.

This leads to an issue that is central to any discussion of religious phenomena. This is the question of the role that reason plays in the clarification of religious experience. The philosopher, in particular, is faced with the problem of rational justification. Just as reason is used to defend beliefs in other areas, it seems that it should be applied here as well. Yet there are difficulties with this viewpoint. The believer posits an object of belief that is totally transcendent. The conventional rational tools do not function as well in this area as they do in others.

In one sense, the philosopher of religion tries to "rationalize" religious claims and experience. His use of reason is directed towards the understanding and clarification of these claims. Although it is generally accepted that his concern is with questions such as those of faith, evil, or immortality, it is also the case that he deals with problems of religious language, argumentation, and justification of belief. Because the question of the relation of reason to religion is central to the philosopher's task, it is this area in which the Existentialists begin their criticisms of traditional philosophy of religion.

Reason and Religion

If reason is applied to religion, there is a danger that the material will be distorted. The attempt to make religious experience intelligible is often used as a substitute for a direct understanding of that experience. When a person is immediately involved in religious phenomena, it is likely that he will have difficulty making his commitment comprehensible to another. In order to philosophize successfully about an experience, the philosopher must live that experience. Therefore, if he finds it easy to explain or reason about religion, the question arises as to how deep his understanding of religion is.

Because the Existentialist starts from his own experience, his approach is unlike that of the traditional philosophers of religion. His experience is significantly different from that of his predecessors; and as a result, his understanding of religious phenomena is different. The Existentialists are less bound to formal religious commitments. They often rebel against the religious institution and prefer to deal with personal growth, rather than with the established forms of belief.

Kierkegaard, in particular, objects to the use of reason to clarify religious experience. The reliance on reason is an attempt to escape subjectivity. Philosophers who are concerned with rational propositions about God focus on the object of religion only. As a result, they are faced with paradoxes. The object of religious experience is a mystery, which reason is totally unable to fathom. Attention should be directed to the experience itself, not to what it claims or to the object that it reveals. Kierkegaard argues that the pagan who worships an idol in a passionate inward way is more religious than the

Christian who reasons objectively about the existence and nature of God.

Kierkegaard's appeal for renewed depth in human experience was developed partly as an attack on Hegel. Hegel's system of pure thought is too rational and abstract. It ignored religious experience. Pure thought excludes passion, and rational proofs ignore the intense subjectivity of religious experience. The inwardness of the experience is its important feature, and inwardness involves self-knowledge, not a knowledge of Hegelian abstractions. To ask Kierkegaard what religious experience is, is like asking a ballerina what she does when she dances. It is impossible to say what the experience is, but one can point to certain characteristics that accompany it. Its essence remains unrevealed, because words carry the seeker away from it. For Kierkegaard, one facet of religious experience is its doubt and uncertainty. The person who claims to know is not religious. Socrates is a hero to Kierkegaard because of his statement that he knew nothing. The uncertainty that constantly accompanies the religious person is reflected in anguish, thus providing the springboard for faith.

But doubt is not enough. There must be passion as well. People without passion are like drunken peasants asleep in a wagon. They let the horses move unguided. A few may wake, but they guide the horses with a weak hand. They have a goal but not enough passion to make their way directly to it. To lead the horses successfully, they must know what it is to take risks and to experience frustration. Passion is the individual's way of making contact with the eternal. If he remains on the level of the rational, he loses control and drops back into drowsiness.

Kierkegaard points out that religious institutions are guilty of objectifying religious beliefs. They often choose to ignore the personal dimension of religious experience. In thinking about God, they lose the individual relationship to God. Pure thought is an abstraction outside of time. The individual, however, is real and living in time. If thought cannot relate to the existing individual, it is useless. And even if it attempts to clarify the individual's experience, it falls short. This is because subjective truth is paradoxical and is often indicated by objective uncertainty. When a person seems to have the least certainty, he may very well have the most truth.

Because reason has been applied excessively to religious experience, philosophy of religion has turned away from religion, not towards it. An outcome of this approach is that philosophers have used God to support their philosophical positions. For Descartes, the existence of God enabled him to prove the existence of the external world. Leibniz' proof of God allowed him to stop the infinite regression of monads. In Berkeley's philosophy, God ensures the existence of the world when man is not there to perceive it. These philosophers put God to the use of knowledge, equating religious beliefs to the finite.

Kierkegaard points out that in all of these positions, God is treated as an object that is known and used by man. If one is to put the relationship in the proper perspective, there must be a shift to a focus on God as a subject and creator. If God is objectified, man thinks of religion much as he does of a physical possession. But possessions are disposable, and as a result, religion becomes dispensable property. The person who objectifies God experiences no real need. He parodies the religious experience without having it directly.

Both Jaspers and Marcel agree with Kierkegaard's stand against the use of reason. In *The Perennial Scope of Philosophy,* Jaspers argues against the view that God's existence can be proven. A major content of faith is the knowledge that God exists, but the attempt to confirm faith by the intellect breaks down. A certainty of God's existence is a premise of intellectual activity. There is no way in which it can be seen as a result. A proved God is no God, since proof without belief is idle intellectual play. Thought can be put to the service of belief, but it cannot create it.

Jaspers does not reject reason altogether as a tool in religious experience. Reason is necessary for communication. The philosopher of religion can put reason to use in the exploration of the polarities that emerge in religious texts. If the

Bible is read literally, it is a mass of contradictions. The philosopher, using his reason, can push behind these contradictions to discover the truths that they .reveal. But reason is a tool only. If the philosopher extends his use of reason to the point of substituting it for faith, he takes it beyond its proper boundaries and confuses the distinction between philosophy and religion.

Marcel, also, finds the rational proofs of God's existence unsatisfactory. The proofs are useful only when they are already unnecessary. If they are used to support belief that is present, they appear circular. The believer is likely to judge them to be an indirect way of attaining what he has already achieved directly. The attempt at proof is useful to the believer only if it is a way of strengthening his belief. But since it already presupposes belief, it seems to have no important function.

On the other hand, if proofs are used by a believer to try to convince an unbeliever, they are equally unsatisfactory. The attempt to convert the unbeliever through the use of reason degrades religious experience. It suggests that the person who is trying to persuade the unbeliever is certain of something that he feels that the other should be convinced of also. This approach is one in which one person tries to exercise power and control over another. The unbeliever is made to look like a fool, or else like someone who is unnecessarily stubborn. His experience is denied or overlooked by the person who tries to convert him.

Kierkegaard, Jaspers, and Marcel all imply that religious experience cannot be organized rationally. Some of the central tenets of religious faith are paradoxical. The content of religion is not doctrinal because large parts of it cannot be taught. Therefore, man's relationship to it is not primarily an intellectual one. His intellect, of necessity, orders ideas, and religious experience resists any such ordering. Or if the intellect is used, it is after a more fundamental relationship with the transcendent has been established.

Marcel suggests that the relationship with the object of religious experience is participatory. It cannot be expressed in categories any more than experiences with other people can be so expressed. The transcendent Other that is experienced in faith is incorporated into the seeker's being. The object of religious faith is an experienced presence, which is not separate from the believer. Marcel observes that the closest any believer has come to describing this experience is exemplified by the writings of some of the great mystics of the religious traditions.

Jaspers indicates that the awareness of the transcendent is often expressed partially through symbol. The ascent to religious faith can be aided in its first stages by philosophy. But philosophy is rejected as the believer moves to different kinds of communication. Eventually even communication is unnecessary in the forms in which it is ordinarily experienced. All of the conventional modes of existence are surpassed towards an incommunicable illumination.

Through the misuse of reason, then, the movement towards faith can be halted. Theories and proofs have stranded man on one level. Jaspers describes the various kinds of distraction that result. Man is likely to become enmeshed in demonology, in which he posits many gods or even establishes himself as a god. Or he may seek to find a god in the perfect man, rejecting all transcendent contents of faith and deifying the human. Or he can become stranded in total unbelief, in which he establishes no relationship between himself and another. All of these experiences, Jaspers maintains, leave man without hope.

Types of Religious Experience

If reason distorts religious experience, in what terms can religious phenomena be discussed? To some extent, if there is to be any discussion at all, one must use the techniques of rational discourse. In spite of the fact that the Existentialists find the deepest religious experiences incommunicable, they do describe different kinds of religious phenomena, and they try to clarify some of the fundamental religious problems. Traditional approaches are modified, and concrete phenomenological analyses are substituted for the more general discussions of religion. Three such analyses are Kierkegaard's consideration of sin, Jaspers' discussion of immortality, and Marcel's conception of hope. Although these studies do not exhaust the material on religion, they provide characteristic examples of much of the work done by the Existentialists on religious issues.

In *Fear and Trembling,* Kierkegaard suggests that sin is a transitional experience had by a person who is between the ethical and religious stages of development. Its origin is in the ethical stage, where refusing to act according to the universal is unacceptable. But the experience does not remain on the level of the ethical because sin is often accompanied by repentance. For repentance there is no ethical explanation. The individual goes beyond the universal. His experience of guilt at rejecting the categorical imperative leads him into repentance, but once he repents, he does not exist on the ethical level in the same way that he did previously. Repentance introduces a new feature. It has to do with the individual, not with the universal. It is a form of inward experience that takes the person away from the ethical towards the religious.

The experience of sin cannot be reasoned into dogma. The talk about sin, and the attempts to explain it are little more than excuses. They try to convert sin into something negative and innocuous in the expectation that the individual referent of sin will be obscured. But if a person experiences himself as sinful, any explanation only aggravates his condition. Thought erases the seriousness from sin; it by-passes sin as it is experienced. The seriousness of the state of sin lies in the fact that a particular individual is a sinner. For Kierkegaard, this fact is linked to the historical fact of God's existence in time. As man becomes aware of what it means to be man, he experiences himself as sinful.

Most men are too distant from faith even to know what it means to sin. One needs a certain degree of spirit to understand what sin is. In order to sin one must be capable of experiencing despair—despair at being unable to will to be himself. The individual's weakness when confronted with his own possibilities is the beginning of his strength because insofar as he recognizes his weakness, he is capable of repentance. Faced with a weakness of will, a person may only despair further, multiplying his sin. But he also may move towards faith when he begins to recognize and accept the inefficacy of his own powers. He wills to be himself, even though he understands that by his will alone, he can do nothing.

Because sin is an experience that goes beyond the ethical stage, attempts to understand it are contradictory. It is a paradox that becomes real in belief, not through understanding. There cannot be a philosophy or a theology of sin because these would be unable to deal with the incomprehensible aspects of the subject matter. Sin exists as lived experience, known by the concrete individual. It is not planned and cannot be defeated by the will. It is a necessary stage in the individual's growth into faith.

Jaspers' discussion of immortality also starts with a warning against the assumption that man can know or understand the experience. No person has definitive knowledge of what happens after death. Although speculation proliferates, most of it is suspect. Human hopes and frustrations are such that the belief in immortality is often linked to dissatisfaction with the present life rather than any understanding of a future life. Sense experience certainly gives no evidence of the existence of a soul separate from the body. Nor are the attempts at proofs of immortality acceptable. Some people try to shift the emphasis from personal immortality to immortality that is gained through children or creative works. However, these are primarily statements of alternative values rather than successful theories of immortality.

A more satisfactory way of approaching the problem of immortality starts from the view that God's being is sufficient. The conception of the transcendent establishes a boundary beyond which man's thought cannot reach. The next step is to propose that if God exists, man must be important. Man was created with certain features: conscious awareness, the ability to love, and the capability of distinguishing values. These features combine to lead his thoughts towards the idea of immortality. "The manifestations of love and the achieve-

ment of self-conquest bring him to awareness in a reality
that is more than transitorily, empirically real—a reality which
still resounds to the word immortality, for all our human ignorance of it."[3]

Jaspers' conception of immortality is not the traditional
one. He argues that the question of a past or a future existence is not relevant. Immortality should be understood as
man's meeting of eternity within time. This happens when
conscience is fulfilled and when love is experienced. The
individual still exists in time, but one dimension of his
experience goes beyond temporal boundaries. The sensually
and intellectually experienced world is transcended, and the
eternal becomes manifest. Concretely, this experience is hinted
at in certain exalted moments. Immortality exists in fidelity
in action or in trustworthiness. But it is not something that
can be directly known.

One of Jaspers' conclusions from this discussion is that man
is mortal when he exists without love and immortal when
he loves. Immortality is not a natural process, nor does it
just happen. It is achieved in the course of man's growth
towards the ability to love. If his life is loveless and confused,
he falls into a void; he has no grasp of his own immortality
or of that of others. In the attempt to understand immortality, the philosopher is forced to use language. But his insight is not the result of an accumulation of knowledge. Once
he has gained such insight, he no longer asks for evidence
or guarantees. The assurance of immortality is nonobjective.

For Jaspers, then, immortality has little to do with a future
life or with the literal separation of the soul from the body.
It indicates a mode of existence in the present life. It offers
no hope of rewards or punishments. Instead, it entails the
human recognition of the self and others. This recognition is
achieved in moments of self-realization and love. Immortality
is not promised to all people, any more than it is true that
all people sin. It is an experience won by the receptive and
available individual. Through self-discipline he establishes
a life within time that has features that transcend time.

Marcel's discussion of hope begins from an analysis of

everyday uses of the experience of hope. As is the case with conventional views of immortality, conceptions of hope often are sustained on a superficial empirical level. When a person hopes that a friend will appear for lunch, this hope is somewhere between a wish and a belief. It is not an experience that demands much of the person who hopes because the conditions for the satisfaction of his wish lie outside of his being. He calculates the probabilities of whether his friend will appear, and he may experience a slight disappointment if his calculations prove wrong.

But in a deeper sense, hope can refer to the deliverance from a trial. In this case, hope actually constitutes the being of the person who hopes. He hopes to be released from some form of captivity or alienation. He does not necessarily direct his expectations towards or against other people. Nor is he merely being optimistic or defiant. He experiences hope as a fundamental aspect of his entire being. His hope can in no way be separated from himself. It is an overcoming of the temptation to despair. In fact, if this temptation is not present, there can be no hope.

If hope is planned or represented, it cannot be understood. It is not the acceptance of a situation, and yet it cannot be considered resistant nonacceptance either. To resist a situation is to make it even more difficult to hope. In hope, there is self-discipline, but the person who hopes is not tense. He establishes a personal rhythm in which he takes his own time. He accepts the trial that faces him, letting it become an integral part of himself. In hoping, he has confidence that things can change. Often through the very fact of his hoping, he promotes the event hoped for.

For Marcel, the experience of hope cannot be separated from that of intersubjectivity. The person who hopes is the person who loves. Hope only exists when there is an interaction between people. Although hope may be directed towards change in the self, it extends beyond the self towards bonds with others. In hoping for something, an individual helps to prepare the way for the situation hoped for. He exercises a creative power, a power that cuts through time. The person who hopes affirms things that others do not see. A parent may have hopes for a child that seem completely unwarranted to the observer. Yet these hopes could be an instrumental feature in the realization of the child's possibilities.

In situations that are more specifically religious, the believer's hope is the individual response of the creature to his creator. When he despairs, he declares, in effect, that God has withdrawn. He sets up an obstacle to transcendence and despairs of himself as well as of God. If, however, a person hopes for his own transformation, this becomes a movement towards faith. The individual who hopes does not ask for reasons or justifications for his hope. He finds it unnecessary to lay down conditions.

Marcel suggests that hope cannot be separated from the experience of grace. Hope does not depend entirely on the person who hopes. At its foundation is something that is offered to the person, something which he can refuse or deny. If he tries to calculate the results of hoping, he defeats its purpose. This is an attempt to objectify hope, assuming it to be more certain than it is. Hope often moves against the objective predictable world, defeating odds and defying calculations. "Hope is essentially the availability of a soul which has entered intimately enough into the experience of communion to accomplish in the teeth of will and knowledge the transcendent act—the act establishing the vital regeneration of which this experience affords both the pledge and the first-fruits."[4]

There are a number of common features in the discussions of sin, immortality, and hope. The three philosophers agree closely on what constitutes unacceptable characterizations of these experiences. They all argue that although philosophy points to some features of these phenomena, it cannot provide a complete description. A theory of sin, a doctrine of immortality, or a dogma of hope would be useless. Discussion is often only rationalization, the attempt to make these experiences less personal and effective than they are. They are never exhausted by what is said or written about them. Because of their role in the growth of the individual, they resist theological generalizations. They are best characterized by phenomenological analyses that impose on them as few preconceptions as possible.

The three philosophers agree that these experiences cannot be discussed objectively. Findings from a psychology laboratory or the statistics of a sociologist cannot explain sin or despair. The exact components of the experiences remain incomprehensible. There is no way of providing quantitative controls or predicting the effects of hope or of a belief in immortality. Such beliefs do have effects, but they cannot be calculated. The effects are internal, influencing both the believer and the world. But it is impossible to establish precisely under what conditions the effects will operate. The calculating mind is at a loss when confronted with a genuine experience of hope or despair.

These three thinkers do not take conventional theological stands on the experiences discussed. In his analysis of sin, Kierkegaard does not make use of accepted theories of original sin. Jaspers indicates scepticism regarding the doctrine of a future life, and Marcel does not analyze the traditional religious objects of hope. Their mutual avoidance of standard religious positions suggests a common feeling that established doctrine hinders inquiry into religious phenomena. If one begins with an accepted position on sin or immortality, there can be no growth as a result of philosophical investigation. The philosopher can only elaborate principles that are already established.

Also Kierkegaard, Jaspers, and Marcel agree in their emphasis on the subjective rather than on the objective. The concern, in the analysis of sin, is not with specific sins and their relative weight. It is with the effect of sin and repentance on the individual who sins. Similarly the objective rewards that may be provided in a future life are irrelevant to the question of immortality. The emphasis is on the individual's personal attempt to transcend temporal limits through experiences of love. And in the discussion of hope, the issue is not whether the individual will realize exactly the event for which he hopes. The fundamental factor is that of the internal effects of the attitude that a person has when he hopes. In none of these experiences are any claims made about objective truths. Their significance lies in their effect upon the individual.

The experiences all have to do with personal growth and realization. The recognition of sin is a way of transcending a slavish commitment to the ethical stage of life. It is despair lived by the concrete individual in the face of paradoxes. Immortality is an experience of breaking through the empirical world as man understands it. It is linked to love and growth beyond the self. Hope also is connected with love. It may come out of despair, even the despair of sin. Yet it suggests that the individual is moving beyond the ego towards others and towards the Absolute. These experiences are often abbreviated—echoes of something promised.

All of these phenomena are experiences of transcendence. In sin a person transcends indifference and the comfort of the universal. In awareness of immortality he transcends his limits in time. In hope, he moves towards the Absolute by making himself available to a force that he cannot calculate. All of these experiences are mysteries and cannot be fully understood. They are concerned with a meeting of the empirical timebound self with that which is infinite, eternal, and unchanging. They reveal nothing about God, but they indicate a considerable amount about the self and about the possibilities of transcending one's empirical situation.

Finally, all of these experiences involve some form of self-discipline. No person can succeed in having them if he considers them as something that is owed to him or as a natural right. They extend beyond the powers of the human will. But this is not to say that man is not instrumental in bringing them about. The individual is a free agent and can resist all forms of growth. Even to experience sin, a person must assume certain risks. If he risks nothing, his belief is unstable. To hope is to risk the chance that one will not be released from a trial and therefore to confront the possibility of despair. In all these experiences, man opens himself to the unknown, without any guarantee of satisfaction or relief. The self-discipline that is necessary prepares the individual for religious experience but keeps him from demanding or objectifying this experience.

The examination of the conceptions of sin, immortality, and hope reveal that the Existentialists do not have, strictly speaking, philosophies of religion. They are interested in exploring religious phenomena but not in systematizing or explaining these phenomena. The focal point in all of the discussions is the individual's experiences of transcendence. The starting point may be the act of transcending one's immediate empirical state but there is a movement along a spectrum of experiences towards the experience of an absolute Other. In the course of this movement, the self grows apace, but the ego is less evident. The experience of being in the presence of an absolute Other is the experience of faith. Sin, immortality, and hope are all variations on the phenomenon of faith, and each is an attempt to particularize faith. It is out of despair and sin that faith emerges; it is the sense of the immortal that gives content to faith; and it is hope that sustains faith. Ultimately for the three philosophers, these issues cannot be separated.

Religious Faith and the Faith of the Philosopher

The question of faith is of paramount importance to the Existentialists. The focus is not on the history of faith but on the faith of the individual. In dealing with a religion, the philosopher's concern is not primarily with its truth. His attention is directed to the individual's relationship to the objects of belief that he holds. Man's potentiality for faith is the core of religious commitment. Without faith, it is meaningless to speak of religious experience at all.

Kierkegaard, Jaspers, and Marcel all agree that faith is not a result of scientific inquiry. It is not something that can be analyzed and acquired. The man who seeks faith seeks something that his intellect cannot control. Kierkegaard claims that

> rather is it the case that in this voluminous knowledge, this certainty that lurks at the door of faith and threatens to

> devour it, he is in so dangerous a situation that he will need
> to put forth much effort in great fear and trembling, lest he
> fall a victim to the temptation to confuse knowledge with
> faith.[5]

If faith is reduced to knowledge, it becomes opinion and is
no longer a living reality. As opinion, it is something claimed
or maintained, held against others. Faith is lived in a way
that opinion is not. Opinions waver while faith remains
constant.

Jaspers observes that any claim to exclusivity on the part
of the believer is unwarranted. The contents of faith are far
from being propositions that are universally true. When exclusivity is stressed, fanaticism is substituted for faith. The
transcendent is replaced by the particular, and dogma is
introduced. The major role that reason can play in the discussion of faith is to indicate situations in which faith is
warped or altered to justify dogma or theology. Reason cannot replace faith, but it can criticize its false forms.

Jaspers contends that faith is the act by which the individual becomes conscious of transcendence. A condition of
this awareness is man's freedom. As he experiences the transcendent, he also undergoes inner unification. It is the very
force of his subjective conviction that makes it possible for
him to recognize the transcendent. As man judges himself,
he hears the voice of God through his judgment. At no time
is faith separate from the growth and transformation of the
self.

Marcel's conception of faith resembles that of Jaspers. He
remarks that the affirmation of God's existence cannot be
separated from the existence of free beings who understand
their role as creatures. Faith in God is connected to fidelity
to oneself, the fidelity expressed in the response to an inner
call. This can be understood as a recognition of the appeal
of conscience. Faith is most real when it issues from a person's
entire being. He fully responds to an invitation, a response
made possible by grace. The believer experiences himself as
part of a larger reality that encompasses him. Faith is the
unceasing witness to this reality.

Of all the Existentialists, it is Kierkegaard who discusses faith in most detail. He proposes that faith is the contradiction between the infinite passion of the person's inwardness and objective uncertainty. It is because one cannot grasp the object of faith objectively that he must have faith. Faith occurs when this paradox is confronted. At the moment when a person realizes that he cannot grasp eternal truth, faith arises. Faith is rooted in contradiction, based in the absurd. It cannot be safeguarded by objective inquiry, nor can it be made clear.

In *Fear and Trembling* Kierkegaard offers Abraham as the example of the knight of faith. At the time when he obeys the command to sacrifice Isaac, Abraham stands as the man who most understands the meaning of faith. There are many ways in which Abraham could act. He could tell his son that the sacrifice is his will alone, not the will of God. In this way, Isaac would not blame God. Or Abraham could obey the command, losing all joy in his religion. Or he could commit the act but live a life of guilt. Yet none of these things happen. They are possible reactions to the command, but if Abraham were to choose them, he would remain an ordinary man.

That which makes Abraham different is the fact that he abandons understanding for faith. His reaction is neither aesthetic nor ethical; it is religious. He moves to the edge of the possible and risks all that he has. There are many ways in which he could risk less. He could decide to spare his son in order to save his wife's feelings. Or he could start up the mountain, but forget the knife. He could look around for a ram upon reaching the top of the mountain. But again, none of these ways are taken. Abraham, because he risks everything, experiences the anguish that accompanies faith. He is in no way assured of the outcome and can understand nothing of God's command. But because he experiences the love of God as incommensurable with human realities, he is prepared to carry out the sacrifice.

Kierkegaard points out that for most men, life is a matter of resignation, not of faith. A lesser man than Abraham would be able to carry out the sacrifice, but his attitude would be one of resignation, rather than joy. He would remember the knife and offer no excuses, but his act would be done out of bitterness. Even if he were to retain his son, the resentment would remain. Having been pushed to the extreme of sorrow, he would bear an ineradicable scar. In Abraham, however, there is a double movement. He carries out the command and experiences anguish, but he is able to retain Isaac with joy. Although at one stage he loses everything, at the next stage he regains all that is lost, and he exists on the same level that he did before receiving God's command. He moves from the finite to the infinite and then back to the finite. There is no external sign of what he has undergone. Whereas the man of resignation bears the scar of the tragic hero, the knight of faith looks like an ordinary man. He goes through suffering and anguish but there are no indications.

According to Kierkegaard, the realm of faith is paradoxical. In this realm, the believer goes beyond the ethical demands that are made of him. He even transcends the commands made to him by his religion. He exists with a constant awareness of the unpredictable. In realizing a direct encounter with the Absolute, there is no law that the knight of faith can follow. He is unable to control his experience, and he gives up any hope that others will understand him. He does not explain or justify his actions. Although he may try to speak, his words have no meaning for others, because his actions are totally unintelligible by human standards. His experience can neither be concealed nor revealed.

There are a few signposts in the journey towards faith. On the one hand, the man of faith finds that his insistent individualism becomes merged with a growing sense of the Absolute. He realizes the Absolute through his particular experience. He stands alone in this experience and lives in silence. In the course of his growth towards the Absolute, the believer goes beyond everyday moral requirements. He is different from others but indistinguishable. His difference is internal, a change in attitude and a movement towards increased inwardness. Yet to the people around him, the changes are unnoticeable.

On the other hand, the man of faith experiences increased depths of intersubjectivity. He says "Thou" to God. He moves away from himself towards the transcendent, and his individual powers of being become absorbed. As he opens up to communication, the ego drops away, and all consciousness refers to the transcendent. At this point, the philosopher has nothing to say. His job of clarification has long since been completed, and the tools of reason and thought are cast aside.

There is, perhaps, a kind of faith peculiar to the philosopher. This is not identical to religious faith, but certain parallels can be found. This faith does not exclude reason, since it is, in part, faith in the Socratic vision. The attempt on Socrates' part to goad the sleeping reason into action is admired by all of the Existentialists. The commitment of the philosopher is a commitment to free inquiry. He too experiences risk and anguish and yet moves out of these experiences into continued investigation.

The philosopher is unable to posit an object of his faith. The outcome of his exploration is often unclear. As soon as a goal is established, it becomes unsatisfactory, because to achieve the goal is to end inquiry. Here also faith is a subjective attitude more than a commitment to clearly established objects. The philosopher has faith in a method but not in a specified subject matter. The subject matter remains in large part unknown, unfolding as the method is used. In addition, the faith of the philosopher is a faith in communication. Although some of the Existentialists suggest that at a certain point communication is transcended, as philosophers they rely on the assumption that they can communicate their insights about experience. One component of this faith is the acceptance of silence as a mode of communication. Although words are the foremost tool of the philosopher, they are extended to indicate the directions in which they cannot operate. They point to experiences that cannot be expressed and that at the same time lose none of their importance.

Finally, the philosopher seems to have faith in refusal and alienation. The refusal is directed against any position or attitude that has become fixed and then imposed on others. It is the refusal to accept objective classification of people and events. The refusal is made in the name of a conception of freedom. If man is free, then no preconceptions about his nature and performance are acceptable. He builds his own commitments and responsibilities and need accept no substitute for his own choices.

But how can there be faith in alienation? Insofar as a person becomes part of an establishment, he loses the sense of his role as a philosopher. For the philosopher, the dialogue can never stop. He is committed to a form of homelessness. He stands by a conviction that he will never achieve his goals. What Sartre describes as a fact of the human condition becomes an object of faith. Not only is it the case that man is always alienated from his possibilities, it also becomes part of his being as a philosopher to accept this alienation. The horizon always recedes as he approaches it. If he were to catch up with it, he would no longer be a seeker.

The ultimate faith of the philosopher is faith in himself. His belief in his enterprise is a belief in the significance of his own experience. He starts his inquiry with that experience because of his conviction that his understanding of others and the world begins with an understanding of himself. Critics argue that this conviction is unjustifiable, and that in the name of philosophical inquiry, the Existentialists merely glorify their own personal idiosyncrasies. The final question that is raised to the Existentialists, then, is the question of whether faith in their unique brand of philosophy is warranted.

8

Conclusion

Criticisms From Within

Some important criticisms of Existentialism come from within the movement itself. There is considerable difference in the approaches taken by the Existentialists. The diversity of backgrounds and temperaments makes it unrealistic to expect agreement on every issue. Thus far, the similarities of the positions have been stressed intentionally. However, it is useful to indicate some of the major areas of disagreement.

Sartre's discussions of Heidegger offer an example of internal criticism. Sartre is indebted to Heidegger for many of his ideas, but he takes issue with some aspects of Heidegger's position. In his analysis of the origin of negation, Sartre suggests that Heidegger is mistaken in considering being and nonbeing antagonistic forces. Heidegger places nonbeing outside of the world, excluding it from being. Sartre attacks this position for its assumption that nonbeing originates simultaneously with being. For Sartre, nonbeing is neither exterior to being nor equivalent to it. Nonbeing is not outside of the world; it lies "coiled in the heart of being—like a worm."[1] Being is inhabited by nonbeing.

To illustrate his position, Sartre points out that when a

person walks into a café expecting to meet a friend, he knows immediately if the friend is not there. He experiences the café as a place from which his friend is absent. The missing person is part of the experience of the café; his absence colors the room, the furniture, and the people present. The nonbeing of the friend is not experienced before or after the perception of the café. The absence is sensed at the very moment the café is entered. In fact, it is the person's awareness that his friend is not present that organizes his experience of the café. Sartre maintains that the origin of nonbeing is man, not being. Because man has fissures in his own being, he finds lacks in his world. If the world were to exist without man, there would be only being—a plenitude in which nonbeing would never appear. Being alone cannot give rise to nonbeing. Only man, who experiences gaps in himself, can find absences in the world. Being and nonbeing are not equivalent forces. Nonbeing is a latecomer, introduced by man.

Thus, in Sartre's example, the absence of the friend is established by the person who enters the café. Because of his awareness of fissures in his own being, he finds the café incomplete. His friend is missing. Until he enters the café, this sense of absence does not exist. He introduces it himself by the structure of his expectations. The café, the tables, the patrons—all are sufficient until he enters and looks for his friend. They are now, however, insufficient, experienced as a lack. With this example Sartre illustrates two major points of disagreement with Heidegger. First, nonbeing is not on a par with being. It is created by man, whereas being is not. Second, nonbeing is not exterior to being. Man introduces nonbeing to being. Nonbeing is held within being, even though being is never affected by it. They are not two conflicting forces because being is in no way influenced by nonbeing.

Sartre also finds Heidegger's conception of the other unsatisfactory. Heidegger begins with an attempt to eliminate the view that the relation between the self and others is external. However, he does not succeed, largely because his rejection of the theory of external relations is incomplete. Since he maintains that the fundamental relation with the other is a relation of knowledge, Heidegger is forced to take the view that the other is a limit, externally imposed upon the self.

Sartre suggests that while Heidegger provides an adequate ontology, he is unable to show how concrete relations with others develop. To understand why one person influences another, one must be able to understand concrete human relations. Why is it that one person limits another's possibilities? Why is a particular kind of relationship, such as love or desire, established? Heidegger provides no means for understanding the different ways in which people are conscious of each other. Sartre grants that Heidegger's conception of the other improves upon traditional approaches. For example, Heidegger does not maintain that the self and the other are two entirely separate substances. He eliminates any assumption that selves are autonomous and argues that at the heart of conscious experience the self and the other are related ontologically. Yet in spite of the fact that he disposes of a major barrier to a satisfactory conception of the other, Heidegger is unable to see all of the implications of his position.

Sartre's criticisms of Heidegger are developed within the context of admiration for Heidegger's accomplishments. While Sartre finds Heidegger's views of nonbeing and the other inadequate, he does state that these conceptions have advanced over those of previous philosophers. The conceptions of nonbeing and the other are taken out of the realm of abstraction in which Hegel placed them and are presented as aspects of concrete experience. Heidegger's faults lie not in the direction he takes but in the fact that he does not pursue his thought far enough.

An example of internal criticism that takes a different direction is Marcel's critical discussion of Sartre's philosophy. In this case, the disagreements are more fundamental, partly because of disparities in the religious and political commitments of the two philosophers. Although their criticisms of their philosophical predecessors have much in common, their conclusions about freedom and human action are different. Marcel's rejection of the classification "Existentialist" in favor of "Neo-Socratic" can be construed partly as a wish to be disassociated from Sartre's philosophy.

Marcel feels that while Sartre adequately describes one aspect of human experience, the description is far from complete. Sartre intentionally degrades the individual. Illustrations of bad faith abound in Sartre's writing, but he gives few examples of good faith. According to Marcel, the possibilities of transformation and growth are neglected by Sartre. Marcel points out that "what is serious is that Sartre leaves out of account the extremely important fact that, when a man who is in good faith admits that he is, say, a homosexual or a liar, all he does is to lay down the conditions which, in his estimation, might enable him to transform himself."[2] There is a difference between admitting and denying the existence of a particular trait. If a thief admits to himself that he is a thief, he is not so much in bad faith as he would be if he denied that fact. Because Sartre often suggests that a person is in bad faith no matter how much he struggles against it, there is little allowance for the possibility of self-mastery.

Similar difficulties emerge in Sartre's analysis of love and giving. There is no doubt that human communication often breaks down. But is this to say that all attempts on the part of one person to communicate with another are self-defeating? To say that a true gift is impossible is to argue in the face of conflicting evidence. Marcel points out that there are numerous situations in which a gift is not designed to enslave another. Although a gift can be used in this way, it can also be part of an act of consecrating oneself to another. The gift can acquire unique being for the other, and through giving, genuine communication can be established.

Marcel also is unable to accept Sartre's conception of religion. Sartre wavers between agnosticism and materialism, never allowing for the possibility of authentic transcendence. By denying the existence of grace, Sartre encloses himself in a narrow world of conflicting selves from which there is no escape. Marcel argues that Sartre's work manifests a "rebellious individuality." His world is closed and atrophied, and man has no access to self-realization.

While Marcel considers Sartre's analyses to be brilliant in design and execution, he claims that they do not exhaust the phenomena that they consider. Sartre discusses giving, but only one form of giving. He explores relations with others but considers these relations only in terms of their power to limit or destroy the projects of others. He talks about transcendence, but excludes modes of religious transcendence. Sartre's descriptions of human experience incorporate useful insights, but there are kinds of experience about which he seems to have no understanding whatever. Furthermore, Sartre's description of man aids the forces of degradation in society. By questioning the authenticity of human values, Sartre encourages the dehumanization of man. Sartre's Existentialism operates on the level of materialism, a level on which man sees himself "as the victim of some cosmic catastrophe, flung into an alien universe to which he is bound by nothing."[3] There is no salvation in Sartre's universe, and there is no hope.

Sartre's criticisms of Heidegger and Marcel's criticisms of Sartre are two areas in which disagreements among the Existentialists themselves are pursued at length. For the most part, their critical work is directed against outsiders—the metaphysics and epistemologies of Descartes, the British Empiricists, and the German Idealists. There are cases in which one Existentialist studies or interprets the thought of another, but these studies are pursued within a context of common assumptions. Jaspers' comments on Kierkegaard and Marcel's study of Jaspers, for example, are largely sympathetic to the philosophers under discussion.

Part of the significance of the internal criticisms is the suggestion that the work of the different thinkers develops independently and often from different starting points. The common positions that do emerge appear to be the result of autonomous inquiry. Yet because there is a strand of agreement running through their thought, it could be argued that the most telling criticisms must come from outside of the movement. For this reason, it is useful to present some of the major objections submitted by critics other than the Existentialists themselves.

Criticisms From Without

The criticisms of Existentialism by non-Existentialists take different directions. Some criticisms are directed against specific arguments, some attack positions that the Existentialists hold in common, and some criticize the attitudes that are held. Although criticisms of particular arguments are probably the most important, they entail detailed study of the work of each philosopher. Such a study is beyond the scope of the present discussion. However, some of the general criticisms will be considered here, as illustrative of the range of reaction to Existentialist thought.

One persistent objection focuses on what the critics consider to be pessimistic—the concerns with death, anguish, and despair, emphasizing the negative aspects of human existence. Man is pictured as a being who is unable to give and unable to love. He is repeatedly confronted with the absurdity of his attempts to understand the world. He has no hope and can find no ultimate justification for his ideals. The ways out of frustration are few, and the possibilities of bad faith and inauthenticity are many.

This criticism is directed primarily against Kierkegaard, Heidegger, and Sartre, although some aspects of Jaspers' and Marcel's characterizations of man are also considered pessimistic. A typical example of such criticism is the following comment on Sartre:

> Too frequently in Sartre's pages we have the impression of having stumbled into a room of some dingy left-bank hotel, where we can see only by the light of a single bulb hanging from the ceiling. It casts sharp shadows and throws a glaring light but our friends are hardly recognizable. And undoubtedly such artificial illumination shows us something . . . but equally certain it is that we are under no compulsion of logic or ontology to see only by the light Sartre's categories provide.[4]

It is not argued that the pessimistic view of man is totally unfounded; the critics claim only that there are other aspects of man that are equally important. Man is capable of bad faith, anguish, and degradation, but he is also capable of transcending these states.

If it is argued that not all Existentialists paint the grim picture of man that Sartre does, some critics are likely to expand their comment into a more general criticism. They point out that the Existentialists as a group take their own experiences too seriously. They suppose that by an exposure of their personal feelings and interests, they reveal truths that are universal. Truths may be revealed by such a method, but they are not universally applicable. They are merely insights into the personalities of the writers. For example, when Kierkegaard calls for a return to subjectivity, he is calling for a return to subjective existence modeled after his own experiences. Yet often Kierkegaard's experience seems to border on the pathological. Although his call for a renewal of faith may be warranted, his attack on conventional institutions at times is part of purely personal concerns.

Critics point out that there is a failure to distinguish between problems of psychology and philosophy. It is true that psychological issues have been increasingly important to philosophers, but this is not to say that all distinctions between the two disciplines should be obliterated. Questions of psychological import are useful to the philosopher but only as long as philosophy retains its identity as a distinct discipline. The Existentialists rely too heavily on insights about the state of their own feelings or attitudes without attempting to correct these insights with the tools of philosophical criticism.

This excessive subjectivism points to another attitude that is criticized. Many of the Existentialists find little use for logic or the philosophy of science. Although a number of them discuss the effects of science on human attitudes, they do not deal critically with questions of the method, the tools, or the uses of science. In addition logic is often considered useless. They argue that logic impedes inquiry, allowing the philosopher to sidestep the real questions.

A typical criticism in this vein argues that "Existentialist logic, based on the fallacy of Either/Or, has no use for probability, and so it largely ignores Science, which deals all the time in probabilities and approximations. A philosophy which cannot come to terms with Science is an anachronism in the twentieth century."[5] To abandon the tools of logic and the scientific attitude is to sacrifice the means whereby philosophy clarifies many of its most persistent problems. Since the Existentialists deal critically with the classical issues of metaphysics, epistemology, and value theory, how can they afford to ignore the insights that have been provided in these areas by logical analysis?

This rejection of some of the traditional philosophical tools is reflected in attitudes towards philosophical terminology. Heidegger, Jaspers, and Sartre are frequently attacked for their introduction of an obscure and often incomprehensible terminology. Kaufmann, for example, accuses Heidegger of piling words on top of words, often with no significant result. Although Heidegger presents what seem to be arguments, under analysis they reveal themselves to be repeated statements of a position rather than arguments in defense of that position.[6]

Such criticisms are based on the claim that a philosophical vocabulary should be built with caution. If old terminology can be used, changes are inadvisable. When philosophers introduce a new vocabulary, they imply that their ideas are too novel to be expressed in traditional ways. Yet many of their ideas are continuous with those of their predecessors. It is possible that in their insistence on new terminology, the Existentialists themselves act in bad faith. They pretend to break radically from their past when in fact their roots are deep in that past.

The conviction of some Existentialists that they are producing a new philosophy leads also to misunderstandings about the history of philosophy. Critics accuse them of distorting historical positions. For example, Walter Kaufmann argues that Kierkegaard attributes to Abraham a distinction between the ethical and religious for which there is no evidence in the Old Testament. He also comments that Heidegger's interpretations of the pre-Socratic philosophers are often unreliable and that Jaspers' analysis of Schelling disregards important aspects of Schelling's intellectual development.[7]

It can be argued that the Existentialists manipulate the

figures of the history of philosophy to serve their own purposes. Sartre and Kierkegaard use Hegel largely as an object against which to direct polemical attacks. There is no systematic study of Hegel's philosophy, and only occasionally are there detailed criticisms of particular arguments. History of philosophy is used largely as a foil, not as source material. Even Heidegger, who relies heavily on the Greeks, often takes the latter out of context, using their positions to buttress his own.

Partly because of the subjectivity of their approach, some of the Existentialists acquire what critics believe to be unsatisfactory political commitments. In their introduction to Heidegger's *Question of Being,* the translators claim that Heidegger fails to grasp the full import of man's political, economic, and social experience. On the political and ethical planes, Heidegger's work is empty, a fact that partially explains his temporary affiliation with the Nazi party. Ontological and political dimensions should reveal each other, but in Heidegger's work there is little continuity between the two.[8]

A similar argument has been used against Sartre. His treatment of Marxism has been characterized as "a frantic effort to follow, from a not always safe distance, the twistings and turnings of the Party line."[9] Although Sartre in his philosophy invariably espouses the freedom of the individual, his political ideas suggest at times that personal freedom is a secondary concern. He adjusts his earlier ideas in order to keep them consistent with Marxist doctrine.

One reason for the political commitments of the Existentialists could be the vehemence of their judgments on the present age. Yet these judgments are also subject to criticism. What is the justification for the extremes to which these thinkers go in attacking technology? One critic, in a largely sympathetic study of Marcel, argues:

> Granted that Marcel has not fallen into the absurd error of condemning technics *in toto* and has . . . explicitly recognized their value, is it not peculiar that he devotes so little effort to drawing out their positive contributions? Does he not remind us of those newspaper columnists who will go on record as

> favoring labor unions in principle but devote endless columns
> to denouncing their abuses? [10]

The criticisms of technology do not follow directly from on-tological or axiological principles. They appear to be evalua-tions resulting from private observation. But since the observa-tion is limited at best, it is difficult to see how these judgments on the present age lead directly to specific political com-mitments.

The fact that there is such a variety of political stands suggests that these stands do not have a philosophical foun-dation. The commitments seem to follow from the philoso-phers' personal background and historical situation rather than from extensive insight into the social situation. The social phi-losophies of the Existentialists are often attached to their ontologies without sufficient attempts to relate the two.

The criticisms discussed thus far are largely attacks on atti-tudes, terminology, and assumptions. Critics, however, also raise questions about some of the major conceptions upon which the Existentialists build their philosophies. Three such conceptions are those of the nature of man, freedom, and the subject-object distinction. Most of the Existentialists agree that man does not have a nature. There is no fixed essence that defines man. Instead, he exists in a situation constituted by his freedom. To suggest that man has a determined nature is to assign him an essence to which he must conform, and this view precludes human freedom.

Yet it can be argued that in spite of their claims to the contrary, these thinkers do have a conception of the nature of man. Their theories of the self have many of the earmarks of a view of human nature. When Sartre speaks of man as the being that originates nonbeing and creates values, he char-acterizes man fully as much as if he were to say that man is de-fined as the rational animal. Or when Marcel and Jaspers argue that the self is realized in conjunction with its ability to communicate with others, they suggest that man can be defined equally well as a social animal.

In addition, the quest for being is an experience that the

Existentialists find natural to man. Otherwise how does one explain the obscure "sense" of being to which most of them refer? Also, how is it possible to characterize Sartre's position that all men seek a godlike totality of being except as a trait of human nature? The quest for being seems to be a permanent feature of man's existence, a necessary factor in human self-realization. Those who argue that man's condition invariably includes the experience of anguish also suggest a feature of human nature.

Moreover, the Existentialists describe man's nature with their insistence that man is free. Some maintain that man chooses his freedom, and others argue that man is free whether he chooses to be or not. There are a number of difficulties that surround these conceptions of freedom. One problem is with the meaning of freedom. If all men are free, what does freedom denote? If freedom means choice, there is a similar confusion. Because man cannot refuse to choose, the notion of choice lacks conceptual precision.

Another problem concerns the conception of responsibility that accompanies this view of freedom. If one accepts the view that all men are free, he also accepts the corollary that all men are responsible. They are responsible not only for their own actions but also for the actions of others. Yet if a person is considered responsible for an action over which he has no direct control, the conception of responsibility is weakened. When there is no discrimination between degrees of responsibility, man is provided with an excuse for taking none of his responsibilities seriously.

Although the criticisms of the views of freedom and responsibility focus largely on Sartre's philosophy, the criticism of the Existentialists' treatment of the subject-object distinction attacks a position that all of these philosophers maintain. This position is that the separation of the subject from the object distorts experience and leads to an irresolvable epistemological dualism. In addition, it is claimed that this distinction makes it possible to emphasize objectivity at the expense of subjectivity, leading to techniques of objectification and degradation.

Such a position on subject-object dualism can be criticized

on the following grounds. In their approach to the distinction between the subject and the object, the Existentialists misunderstand the nature and purpose of this distinction. It is introduced in epistemology to characterize the difference that is found between the knower and the thing known. By eliminating the subject-object distinction, the Existentialists are compelled to deal with this difference in other ways. They suggest that instead of the subject and the object, there is a self participating as a presence in the world. But in spite of the change in terminology, the subject-object division persists. The self becomes the subject, and the world, the object.

Moreover, it can be argued that a separation of a subject from an object does not make it impossible to understand the unities of experience. The experience of knowing an object is still one experience had by one person. The object is posited as different from the subject, but this does not imply that the subject is so divided from the object that there is no relation between them. The relationship between them is that of knowledge. There is no barrier between the subject and the object; man still knows his world. The subject-object distinction makes it possible to distinguish between himself and his world.

The conceptions of subject and object provide a means of organizing and dealing with knowledge. The distinction only leads to objectification if the person who makes the distinction prefers to stress objectivity. One can achieve as many insights about the self and subjectivity with the distinction as without it. The attitudes that make dehumanization and degradation possible need not be traced to the clarification of a difference between the knower and the things known. It is more likely that these attitudes are attributable to social and economic conditions rather than to a group of philosophical assumptions.

In summary, the most frequent criticisms focus on both attitude and content. The movement is attacked for its pessimism and for its refusal to recognize positive features in human experience. The Existentialists take their own experience too seriously, confusing philosophy with clinical psychology, and assuming that what is true of themselves personally is also true of all men. Since subjective experience is emphasized, logic and philosophy of science are underestimated. The advances of science are often confused with the dehumanizing attitudes that accompany technological advances. Finally, positions regarding human nature, freedom, and the subject-object distinction by-pass traditional insights, often at the expense of clarification of experience.

If one general criticism can be made, it is that the Existentialists' stands are not rigorously argued. Insights are often presented persuasively, but without the careful examination of presuppositions that is behind any enduring philosophical position. Because many Existentialist positions are supported by important and interesting psychological observations, one finds it easy to leave the soundness of the arguments unquestioned. Yet if these arguments are closely examined, they reveal weaknesses that might be avoided if their authors were to select and use their philosophical tools with more care.

Rejoinders and New Directions

For the most part, the Existentialists do not try to meet the criticisms directed against them. One reason for this reluctance may be the awareness that the critics work from assumptions so different that dialogue is virtually impossible. More important, perhaps, is a feeling that any attempt to answer extensive criticism is futile. Philosophy is in danger of becoming obscured in argumentation at the expense of insight into the fundamental questions. Often these thinkers suggest that they are proposing a method only, one to be used by each individual to clarify his own experience. Since they do not aim at providing a dogmatic philosophical position, the arguments of their critics often miscarry completely.

At the same time, however, not all criticisms can be passed off in this manner. Granted, there is a tentative nature to many of the findings of the Existentialists. Yet in spite of this exploratory approach, philosophical argumentation is used and definite positions are maintained. Many of the criticisms come from philosophers who are in partial sympathy with the movement, and their criticisms are sincere attempts to point to difficulties in assumptions and arguments. To ignore these criticisms completely would be a mistake, since they indicate ways in which the Existentialist position can be strengthened and clarified.

One major issue is the charge of pessimism—the undue focus on man's limits and his frustrations. In answer to this charge, it can be pointed out, first of all, that this characterization does not apply to Marcel and Jaspers. Their writings suggest that while man is restricted by others and by the limits imposed on him by a technologically oriented society, he has at his command numerous means of transcendence. Both Marcel and Jaspers explore a variety of experiences, such as hope, faith and intersubjectivity—experiences that directly implement self-realization.

The attribute of pessimism is applied more frequently to the works of Kierkegaard, Heidegger, and Sartre. Sartre's discussion of this issue in "Existentialism Is a Humanism" can be used to speak for all three. He argues that this criticism takes his view of man out of context. In fact, he proposes a theory of freedom that is based on a broad conception of human potential. Because man makes himself, it is always possible for him to create new values. His values are not presented to him ready-made. He chooses them, and in so doing, he has the power to change his situation.

If anything, then, the philosophy is an optimistic one. It gives priority to questions of conversion and transformation and puts responsibility for values in man's hands. He is not subject to the arbitrary decisions of a capricious god or the immutable conditions of a deterministic view of the nature of man. His anguish and despair result from the awesomeness of his responsibility, not from any sense of futility or lack of control.

But there is still the matter of the concern for death. In the writings of Heidegger, in particular, it is suggested that man lives towards death and must be conscious of his mortality if he is to live authentically. Both Kierkegaard and Sartre consider death to be a major philosophical issue. To deal with this issue, it is useful to recall that one of the aims of the Existentialists is to clarify the human situation. Insofar as man refuses to think about his situation, he blinds himself both to his possibilities and his limits. To consider the issue of death philosophically insignificant is to ignore one of the most irrevocable facts of human existence. The fact that man must die limits all aspects of his life—his projects, his hopes, and his relations with others. The emphasis on death as a limit is less a matter of being pessimistic than one of being realistic. If a central concern of the philosopher is that of the self and self-realization, it is unreasonable to ignore the fact of mortality.

In part, the answer to the accusation of pessimism provides an answer as well to the criticism that the Existentialists are overly subjective in their approach to philosophical issues. Their critics argue that because the Existentialists take their own experience too seriously, they have a tendency to confuse philosophical truths with psychological ones. To this, one reply might be that such criticism indicates a misunderstanding of the goals of philosophy. If philosophy aims at clarification of the human situation, man cannot be excluded.

The use of psychological insights in the development of a philosophical position is not necessarily the result of a confusion regarding the boundaries of the two disciplines. Instead, it is the result of a recognition that the truth about man must be drawn from a variety of sources. The Existentialists maintain that the experience of the individual is the starting point for any discussion of a philosophical issue. The inquirer's own experience is the data that is most readily available to him. To ignore this experience would be to eliminate one of the most obvious sources of philosophical material.

It is maintained, then, that it is artificial to exclude any relevant data from philosophy. If material from literature is applicable, it should be used. If information from the social sciences is available, it too provides source material. And if the data comes from the inquirer's personal experience, this is perhaps the most useful material of all. The conception of philosophy should be broad enough to allow for the inclusion of content that aids understanding, regardless of its source.

But if this position is held, why is so little attention given to logic and the philosophy of science? These are areas relevant to philosophical inquiry, but they are left largely untouched. The Existentialists might return with the argument that, although they respect these disciplines, they are not particularly useful in the study of being, the self, and human values—areas of particular emphasis in their philosophies. Logic has become identified with questions of linguistic usage in the analytic philosophical tradition. For the Existentialists, however, knowledge is related primarily to the self and consciousness, not to the formal structure and uses of language.

Their conceptions of language are one reason for the introduction of new terminology. Language is closely tied to the existence of the self. It cannot be explored without reference to human experience. If terminology were to persist unchanged, this would suggest that man's experiences are not changing. It is true that many of the ideas introduced by the Existentialists have their origins in the history of philosophy, and some of the terminology suggests these origins. But as these ideas are developed, they give evidence of a radical departure from traditional conceptions. If the Existentialists were to retain the conventional philosophical language, the reader's interpretation would be influenced by positions maintained by the philosophers with whom this language is associated. Such associations would damage rather than illuminate their positions.

The Existentialists maintain that they have something to add to philosophy. They are not merely refurbishing old concepts. Their experiences are considerably different from those of their predecessors; as a result of these differences, conceptions such as those of freedom and responsibility undergo a major transformation. This partially explains why they do not offer detailed studies of problems presented by historical philosophical positions. The desire to "destroy" parts of the history of philosophy can be interpreted as a wish to avoid being absorbed by past traditions.

Preoccupation with the past, according to some of them, is a way of sidestepping commitment. Perhaps some of the political commitments of the Existentialists appear hasty, but they exemplify a movement beyond the refusal to take any position whatever. These commitments entail risks, but they are risks consonant with the human situation. Thought and action cannot be sharply separated. Not to act in the light of ideas that commit one to action is to exist inauthentically. The fact that the political affiliations are different speaks in their favor. If they were to take identical positions, this unanimity would suggest that they had abandoned their commitment to independent inquiry.

The views of man's situation and his freedom reflect the Existentialists' wish to free themselves from their philosophical heritage. In their attack on conceptions of the nature of man, they are not arguing that no characteristics can be ascribed to man. There are certain traits that make man's situation what it is. They are maintaining that man himself decides how he will interpret and use these traits. All men create values, but each man chooses the particular attitudes he will take towards his values. The opposition to a fixed theory of human nature focuses on the dogmatic aspects of that position. Nothing compels any person to act in the way that he does. Because of his freedom, he alone directs that action, and he alone is responsible for it.

One of the strongest objections put to Existentialism is directed against the rejection of the subject-object distinction. The Existentialists seem to presuppose this distinction at the very moment they claim to eliminate it. The distinction is an epistemological tool resulting from reflection about the way in which man knows his world. The distinction is rejected in part because it leads to an underestimation of subjectivity. Yet it is difficult to see how the subject-object distinction can be held responsible for objectification. The concern for self-realization can be developed satisfactorily within the context of a distinction between the self and the objects of its knowledge.

Some of the Existentialists suggest that a theory of participation can be substituted for a theory of knowledge, replacing the subject-object dualism with a view that does not isolate man from his world. Yet this rejoinder presupposes that the distinction between the subject and the object is reflected in an experienced break between the two components of knowledge. Those who maintain the subject-object distinction could argue that this is not in fact the case. The distinction is part of a description of the knowing process; it is not identical to the experience of knowing.

Of the numerous criticisms that have been made, the criticisms regarding the subject-object distinction appear to be among the strongest. Many of the other criticisms reflect the critics' lack of sympathy with assumptions and attitudes rather than with inadequacies in argumentation. It is partly for this reason that the Existentialists often ignore their critics instead of dealing with them directly.

In many ways, Existentialism stands outside the mainstream of philosophy. It has had profound influence beyond the philosophical profession. Although serving as catalytic agents within the history of philosophical thought, some of the Existentialists prefer to dissociate themselves from professional philosophy. They are not writing philosophies that they expect to endure permanently. Even Sartre, who offers one of the more systematic philosophical positions, indicates that he thinks that his own philosophy will lose importance once man's social and economic situation alters. He views his work as a transitional effort that he expects to have immediate effect but one that makes no claims for philosophical immortality.

To write a philosophy for all time is for the Existentialists as idle a dream as man's desire to be God. Philosophy is one expression of human wonder and curiosity, and it is as variable as the expressions of wonder and curiosity. Some of these philosophers consider themselves Socratic gadflies. Their task is to question and to remind, not to bequeath a body of dogma to subsequent philosophers. To some extent, they accomplish what they set out to achieve. They raise questions that puzzle their contemporaries and that are instrumental in pointing out the role that the unique experience of the individual plays in providing philosophical insights. Although some of their characterizations of the human situation are questionable, men of the present age recognize themselves in many of the descriptions. The picture is often unflattering, even disturbing, but to some it has come to seem increasingly accurate.

One of the goals of the Existentialists is to establish new directions for philosophy. It is not possible to predict exactly what directions Existentialism will take, but one can speculate that it may move towards more work in social and political philosophy. The increasing demands that the contemporary political situation makes on the citizen suggests that Sartre's attempt to produce a viable social philosophy may be followed by similar projects with an Existentialist orientation.

To philosophers generally, one legacy of the Existentialists is a renewed interest in the way in which philosophical ideas are presented. Although the Existentialists contribute their share of unwieldy prose, there is more innovation in philosophical method than can be found in any other contemporary philosophical movement. They feel no hesitation in drawing material from their personal journals, their plays, or their fictional writings to clarify their philosophical positions.

Perhaps most important is the ability on the part of the Existentialists to combine the rigors of philosophical method with problems of intense contemporary and personal concern. This approach makes them vulnerable to criticism for their excessive subjectivity; yet it also keeps philosophy in the public arena. The Existentialists admire Socrates for this very reason. His philosophy was not primarily a body of thought. It was an exploration of the issues that emerge directly out of man's personal endeavors to understand and control his world. To the extent that they endorse this conception of philosophy, the Existentialists can fairly be called neo-Socratics. Philosophy begins from the personal and historical situation in which one finds himself, and philosophical inquiry is pursued as long as man exists in that situation.

Notes

CHAPTER I

[1] A group of essays by Americans on the relationship between Existentialism and psychology can be found in *Existential Psychology,* Rollo May, ed. (New York: Random House, 1961). An introduction to Tillich's thought is available in his *The Courage To Be* (New Haven: Yale University Press, 1952). For a discussion of Tillich's relation to other contemporary theologians, see Ernst Breisach, *Introduction to Modern Existentialism* (New York: Grove Press, Inc., 1962), pp. 136–150.

[2] Two examples of studies that explore these implications are: Robert Cumming, "The Literature of Extreme Situations," in *Aesthetics Today,* ed. Morris Philipson (Cleveland: Meridian Books, 1961), pp. 377–412; and Hazel Barnes, *Humanistic Existentialism: The Literature of Possibility* (Lincoln: The University of Nebraska Press, 1959), *passim.*

[3] The phrase, "the crowd is untruth," is taken from the essay, "The Individual," in Søren Kierkegaard, *The Point of View for My Work as an Author: A Report to History,* trans. Walter Lowrie (New York: Harper & Brothers, 1962), pp. 109–120.

[4] Jean-Paul Sartre, "Existentialism Is a Humanism," in *Existentialism: From Dostoevsky to Sartre,* Walter Kaufmann, ed. (Cleveland: Meridian Books, 1956), pp. 287–311.

[5] Søren Kierkegaard, *Fear and Trembling and the Sickness Unto Death,* trans. Walter Lowrie (New York: Doubleday & Company, Inc., 1954), pp. 22–25.

[6] Søren Kierkegaard, *The Journals of Kierkegaard,* trans. Alexander Dru (New York: Harper & Brothers, 1959), p. 98.

[7] Kierkegaard, *Journals,* p. 53.

[8] Karl Jaspers, *Man in the Modern Age,* trans. Eden and Cedar Paul (New York: Doubleday & Company, Inc., 1957), p. 176.

⁹ José Ortega y Gasset, *What is Philosophy?* (New York: W. W. Norton & Company, Inc., 1960), p. 66.

¹⁰ Kaufmann, *Existentialism,* p. 138.

¹¹ Kierkegaard writes, "There is a bird called the stormy petrel, and that is what I am, when in a generation storms begin to gather, individuals of my type appear." *Journals,* p. 95.

¹² For a more detailed analysis of Husserl's contributions to the phenomenological movement, see the volume on phenomenology in this series.

¹³ Martin Heidegger, *Being and Time,* trans. John Macquarrie and Edward Robinson (New York: Harper & Brothers, 1962), p. 50. A general discussion of method can be found in *Being and Time,* pp. 49–63.

¹⁴ See Herbert Spiegelberg, *The Phenomenological Movement: A Historical Introduction* (The Hague: Martinus Nijhoff, 1960), II, p. 409.

¹⁵ Gabriel Marcel, *The Existential Background of Human Dignity* (Cambridge, Massachusetts: Harvard University Press, 1963), p. 96.

¹⁶ *Being and Time,* p. 50.

¹⁷ *Being and Time,* p. 62.

¹⁸ Jean-Paul Sartre, *Being and Nothingness: An Essay on Phenomenological Ontology,* trans. Hazel E. Barnes (New York: Philosophical Library, 1956), p. 107.

CHAPTER II

¹ *Point of View,* p. 129.

² Martin Heidegger, *An Introduction to Metaphysics,* trans. Ralph Manheim (Garden City, New York: Doubleday & Company, Inc., 1961), p. 1. Manheim has used "essents" as a translation of *Seiendes.* There are a number of alternative translations of this word by different translators of Heidegger. The least awkward seems to be the word "entity" used by the translators of *Sein und Zeit.* See *Being and Time,* p. 22, footnote, for a discussion of the translation of this word.

³ *Being and Nothingness,* p. 4.

⁴ Gabriel Marcel, *Présence et immortalité* (Paris: Flammarion, 1959), p. 21. This question is formulated most succinctly in this untranslated work but is posed in other works as well. See, for example, the essay "On the Ontological Mystery" in his *The Philosophy of Existentialism,* trans. Manya Harari (New York: The Citadel Press, 1961).

⁵ Cf. John Locke, *An Essay Concerning Human Understanding;* George Berkeley, *A Treatise Concerning the Principles of Human Knowledge;* David Hume, *An Enquiry Concerning Human Understanding;* and Immanuel Kant, *Critique of Pure Reason.*

⁶ Martin Heidegger, *Existence and Being,* ed. Werner Brock (Chicago: Gateway, 1949), p. 325.

[7] For a literary evocation of the reaction of man to being-in-itself, see Jean-Paul Sartre, *Nausea,* trans. Lloyd Alexander (New York: New Directions, 1964).

[8] Karl Jaspers, *Truth and Symbol,* trans. Jean T. Wilde, William Kluback, and William Kimmel (New Haven: College and University Press, 1959), p. 22.

[9] Marcel appears to be influenced here by Hegel's discussion of the conflict of selves, or "Lordship and Bondage." See G. W. F. Hegel, *The Phenomenology of Mind,* trans. J. B. Baillie (2nd ed., New York: The Macmillan Company, 1955), pp. 228–240.

[10] Gabriel Marcel, *Being and Having: An Existentialist Diary,* trans. Katherine Farrer (New York: Harper & Row, 1965), p. 165.

CHAPTER III

[1] Martin Heidegger, *Discourse On Thinking,* trans. John M. Anderson and E. Hans Freund (New York: Harper & Row, 1966), p. 50.

[2] *Introduction to Metaphysics,* p. 5.

CHAPTER IV

[1] *Fear and Trembling,* p. 86.

[2] Sartre's play, "No Exit," is a vivid dramatic presentation of his conception of the weight of the past. See *No Exit and Three Other Plays,* trans. Stuart Gilbert and Lionel Abel (New York: Vintage Books, 1946).

[3] *Being and Time,* p. 443.

[4] Karl Jaspers, *Reason and Existenz,* trans. William Earle (New York: Noonday Press, 1955), p. 106.

[5] *Existence and Being,* p. 309.

[6] *Reason and Existenz,* p. 92.

[7] Marcel's theory of intersubjectivity suggests features of the conception of community developed by the American philosopher, Josiah Royce. See Gabriel Marcel, *Royce's Metaphysics,* trans. Virginia and Gordon Ringer (Chicago: Henry Regnery Company, 1956).

[8] *Being and Time,* p. 167.

[9] *Being and Nothingness,* p. 256.

CHAPTER V

[1] For a more detailed distinction between normative ethics and meta-ethics, see Richard T. Garner and Bernard Rosen, *Moral Philosophy: A Systematic Introduction to Normative Ethics and Meta-Ethics* (New York: The Macmillan Company, 1967), pp. 213–216.

[2] "Jean-Paul Sartre s'explique sur 'Les Mots'," (an interview conducted with Sartre by Jacqueline Piatier), *Le Monde,* April 18, 1964, p. 13.

[3] Simone de Beauvoir, *The Ethics of Ambiguity,* trans. Bernard Frechtman (New York: Philosophical Library, 1948), p. 51.

[4] Søren Kierkegaard, *Either/Or,* trans. Walter Lowrie (2 vols; New York: Doubleday & Company, Inc., 1959), II, p. 252.

[5] Quoted in Simone de Beauvoir, *Force of Circumstance,* trans. Richard Howard (New York: G. P. Putnam's Sons, 1965), p. 199.

[6] *Existence and Being,* p. 343.

[7] This play has not yet been translated. It was originally published in French in conjunction with "On the Ontological Mystery," which is translated in *Philosophy of Existentialism.* A number of Marcel's other plays present similar themes. See Gabriel Marcel, *Three Plays: A Man of God, Ariadne, The Funeral Pyre,* trans. Rosalind Heywood, Marjorie Gabain (London: Secker & Warburg, 1952).

[8] Heidegger, *Being and Time,* p. 223.

[9] For specific examples of how existential psychoanalysis uses this method, see Rollo May, Ernest Angel, and Henri F. Ellenberger, eds., *Existence: A New Dimension in Psychiatry and Psychology* (New York: Basic Books, Inc., 1958).

[10] *Being and Nothingness,* p. 476.

[11] A number of recent philosophers have presented arguments against this view of determinism, pointing out that determinism need not exclude a conception of human freedom. See Bernard Berofsky, ed., *Free Will and Determinism* (New York: Harper & Row, 1966), Section 2.

[12] *Being and Nothingness,* p. 556.

CHAPTER VI

[1] Gabriel Marcel, *Philosophical Fragments: 1909–1914* and *The Philosopher and Peace,* trans. Lionel A. Blain (Notre Dame, Indiana: University of Notre Dame Press, 1965), p. 11.

[2] See Chapter V, footnote 2.

[3] Jean-Paul Sartre, *Literature and Existentialism,* trans. Bernard Frechtman (New York: The Citadel Press, 1962), p. 63.

[4] The material for this section is drawn from the following three works: Jaspers, *Man in the Modern Age;* Søren Kierkegaard, *The Present Age* and *Of the Difference Between a Genius and an Apostle,* trans. Alexander Dru (New York: Harper & Row, 1962); and Gabriel Marcel, *Man Against Mass Society,* trans. G. S. Fraser (Chicago: Gateway, 1962). Although the "present age" is a different historical period in the case of each of the three philosophers, the arguments are so close that the conclusions can be grouped together into a single position.

[5] Kierkegaard, *Present Age,* p. 35.

[6] For a discussion of the misuse of the authority of the state, see

Karl Jaspers, *The Question of German Guilt,* trans. E. B. Ashton (New York: Capricorn Books, 1961).

[7] *Present Age,* pp. 73–76.

[8] For a detailed discussion of this position, see Karl Jaspers, *The Origin and Goal of History,* trans. Michael Bullock (New Haven: Yale University Press, 1953).

[9] The material discussed here is taken from Jean-Paul Sartre, *Search for a Method,* trans. Hazel E. Barnes (New York: Alfred A. Knopf, 1963). The major portion of Sartre's *Critique* is not yet translated. Some sections, however, are translated and anthologized in Robert Denoon Cumming, ed., *The Philosophy of Jean-Paul Sartre* (New York: The Modern Library, 1966).

[10] This essay can be found in Jean-Paul Sartre, *Literary and Philosophical Essays,* trans. Annette Michelson (New York: Collier Books, 1962).

CHAPTER VII

[1] *Philosophy of Existentialism,* p. 44.

[2] Kaufmann, *Existentialism,* p. 311.

[3] Karl Jaspers, *Philosophy and the World,* trans. E. B. Ashton (Chicago: Gateway, 1963), p. 137.

[4] Gabriel Marcel, *Homo Viator: Introduction to a Metaphysic of Hope,* trans. Emma Craufurd (New York: Harper & Brothers, 1962), p. 67.

[5] Søren Kierkegaard, *Concluding Unscientific Postcript to the Philosophical Fragments,* trans. David F. Swenson and Walter Lowrie (Princeton University Press, 1944), p. 30.

CHAPTER VIII

[1] *Being and Nothingness,* p. 21.

[2] *Philosophy of Existentialism,* p. 69.

[3] *Philosophy of Existentialism,* p. 102.

[4] William Earle, James M. Edie, and John Wild, *Christianity and Existentialism* (Evanston: Northwestern University Press, 1963), p. 90.

[5] Hector Hawton, *The Feast of Unreason* (London: Watts & Co., 1952), p. 214.

[6] See Walter Kaufmann, *From Shakespeare to Existentialism* (New York: Doubleday & Company, Inc., 1960), Ch. 17.

[7] *From Shakespeare to Existentialism,* pp. 177, 359, 380.

[8] Martin Heidegger, *The Question of Being,* trans. William Kluback and Jean T. Wilde (New Haven: College & University Press, 1958), pp. 12–16.

[9] Cumming, *The Philosophy of Jean-Paul Sartre,* p. 38.

[10] Kenneth T. Gallagher, *The Philosophy of Gabriel Marcel* (New York: Fordham University Press, 1962), p. 150.

Bibliography

Primary Sources: Major Works

The following books are the major works used in this study. For more inclusive bibliographies of the writings of the individual authors, see the section on bibliographies below.

Heidegger, Martin. *Being and Time.* Trans. John Macquarrie and Edward Robinson. New York: Harper & Brothers, 1962.
_____. *Discourse on Thinking.* Trans. John M. Anderson and E. Hans Freund. New York: Harper & Row, 1966.
_____. *Existence and Being.* ed. Werner Brock. Chicago: Gateway, 1949.
_____. *An Introduction to Metaphysics.* Trans. Ralph Manheim. Garden City, New York: Doubleday & Company, Inc., 1961.
Jaspers, Karl. *Man in the Modern Age.* Trans. Eden and Cedar Paul. New York: Doubleday & Company, Inc., 1957.
_____. *The Perennial Scope of Philosophy.* Trans. Ralph Manheim. New York: Philosophical Library, 1949.
_____. *Reason and Existenz.* Trans. William Earle. New York: Noonday Press, 1955.
_____. *Truth and Symbol.* Trans. Jean T. Wilde, William Kluback, and William Kimmel. New Haven: College and University Press, 1959.
Kierkegaard, Søren. *Concluding Unscientific Postcript to the Philosophical Fragments.* Trans. David F. Swenson and Walter Lowrie. Princeton: Princeton University Press, 1944.
_____. *Either/Or.* Vol. I. Trans. David F. Swenson and Lillian Marvin Swenson. Vol. II. Trans. Walter Lowrie. New York: Doubleday & Company, Inc., 1959.
_____. *Fear and Trembling* and *The Sickness Unto Death.* Trans. Walter Lowrie. New York: Doubleday & Company, Inc., 1954.
_____. *The Point of View For My Work as an Author: A Report to History.* Trans. Walter Lowrie. New York: Harper & Brothers, 1962.
_____. *The Present Age* and *Of the Difference Between a Genius and an Apostle.* Trans. Alexander Dru. New York: Harper & Row, 1962.

Marcel, Gabriel. *Being and Having: An Existentialist Diary.* Trans. Katherine Farrer. New York: Harper & Row, 1965.
_____. *Man Against Mass Society.* Trans. G. S. Fraser. Chicago: Gateway, 1962.
_____. *The Mystery of Being.* Vol. I: *Reflection and Mystery.* Trans. G. S. Fraser. Vol. II: *Faith and Reality.* Trans. René Hague. Chicago: Gateway, 1960.
_____. *The Philosophy of Existentialism.* Trans. Manya Harari. New York: The Citadel Press, 1961.
Sartre, Jean-Paul. *Being and Nothingness: An Essay in Phenomenological Ontology.* Trans. Hazel E. Barnes. New York: Philosophical Library, 1956.
_____. *Literature and Existentialism.* Trans. Bernard Frechtman. New York: The Citadel Press, 1962.
_____. *Search for a Method.* Trans. Hazel E. Barnes. New York: Alfred A. Knopf, 1963.

Primary Sources: Additional Works

These works are not, for the most part, of a technical philosophical nature. They are helpful to read in conjunction with the philosophical works cited above, since they can be used as concrete illustrations of a number of the major themes of Existentialism. References to other relevant works can be found in footnotes to the text.

Barnes, Hazel E. *An Existentialist Ethics.* New York: Alfred A. Knopf, 1967.
Berdyaev, Nicolas. *The Fate of Man in the Modern World.* Trans. Donald A. Lowrie. Ann Arbor: The University of Michigan Press, 1961.
Buber, Martin. *I and Thou.* Second ed. Trans. Ronald Gregor Smith. New York: Charles Scribner's Sons, 1958.
Bugbee, Henry G., Jr. *The Inward Morning: A Philosophical Exploration in Journal Form.* New York: Collier Books, 1961.
Camus, Albert. *The Myth of Sisyphus and Other Essays.* Trans. Justin O'Brien. New York: Vintage Books, 1955.
Nietzsche, Friedrich. *Beyond Good and Evil: Prelude to a Philosophy of the Future.* Trans. Walter Kaufmann. New York: Vintage Books, 1966.
Sartre, Jean-Paul. *The Words.* Trans. Bernard Frechtman. New York: Fawcett Publications, Inc., 1964.

Bibliographies

The following books and articles contain reasonably complete bibliographies of primary and secondary materials for Kierkegaard, Jaspers, Sartre, Heidegger, and Marcel.

Hollander, Lee M., ed. *Selections From the Writings of Kierkegaard.* New York: Doubleday & Company, Inc., 1960.
Schilpp, Paul Arthur, ed. *The Philosophy of Karl Jaspers.* New York: Tudor Publishing Company, 1957.
Schrader, George Alfred, Jr., ed. *Existential Philosophers: Kierkegaard to Merleau-Ponty.* New York: McGraw-Hill Book Company, 1967.

Spiegelberg, Herbert. *The Phenomenological Movement: A Historical Introduction.* 2 vols. The Hague: Martinus Nijhoff, 1960.
Wenning, Gerald G. "Works By and About Gabriel Marcel," *The Southern Journal of Philosophy,* IV, No. 2 (Summer, 1966), 82–96.

Anthologies

Because of the increasing availability of primary materials on Existentialism, selections in anthologies provide a convenient introduction to the works of the major authors. The books edited by Kaufmann and by Wilde and Kimmel are general anthologies. The others present basic writings of specific authors. The writings of Heidegger, Jaspers, and Marcel have not yet been satisfactorily anthologized.

Bretall, Robert, ed. *A Kierkegaard Anthology.* New York: The Modern Library, 1946.
Cumming, Robert Denoon, ed. *The Philosophy of Jean-Paul Sartre.* New York: The Modern Library, 1966.
Kaufmann, Walter, ed. *Existentialism From Dostoevsky to Sartre.* Cleveland: Meridian Books, 1956.
Wilde, Jean T. and Kimmel, William, ed. *The Search For Being: Essays From Kierkegaard to Sartre on the Problems of Existence.* New York: The Noonday Press, 1962.

Secondary Sources: Periodicals

Almost all of the major philosophical periodicals publish articles on Existentialism. The following journals are devoted exclusively to topics in Existentialism and Phenomenology.

Journal of Existentialism. (Formerly *Journal of Existential Psychiatry*).
Review of Existential Psychology and Psychiatry. (Published by the Association of Existential Psychology and Psychiatry).

Secondary Sources: Books

Secondary sources on Existentialism are extremely numerous. This list covers one or more expository secondary source for each major figure who has been discussed in this book. Two useful general secondary sources that include more than one philosopher are the books by Schrader and Spiegelberg cited above. Schrader includes contemporary essays on all of the major Existentialists. Spiegelberg's study is presented as a history of Phenomenology, but it also offers an extensive introduction to Heidegger, Marcel, and Sartre.

A. *Heidegger*

Barrett, William. *What is Existentialism?* New York: Grove Press, Inc., 1964, Part II.

King, Magda. *Heidegger's Philosophy: A Guide to His Basic Thought.* New York: The Macmillan Company, 1964.

B. *Jaspers*

There is no complete study of Jaspers' thought available in English. The major secondary source on Jaspers' work is the group of essays in the volume edited by Schilpp, cited above.

C. *Kierkegaard*

Lowrie, Walter. *Kierkegaard.* 2 vols. New York: Harper & Brothers, 1962.

D. *Marcel*

Gallagher, Kenneth T. *The Philosophy of Gabriel Marcel.* New York: Fordham University Press, 1962.

E. *Sartre*

In the following two works, Desan analyzes in detail Sartre's *Critique of Dialectical Reason* and *Being and Nothingness.*

Desan, Wilfrid. *The Marxism of Jean-Paul Sartre.* New York: Doubleday & Company, Inc., 1966.
_____. *The Tragic Finale: An Essay on the Philosophy of Jean-Paul Sartre.* New York: Harper & Row, 1960.

Index